ASHE Higher Education Report: Volume 36, Number 2
Kelly Ward, Lisa E. Wolf-Wendel, Series Editors

Partnerships and Collaborations in Higher Education

Pamela L. Eddy

D1202643

Partnerships and Collaborations in Higher Education
Pamela L. Eddy
ASHE Higher Education Report: Volume 36, Number 2
Kelly Ward, Lisa E. Wolf-Wendel, Series Editors

ISSN 1551-6970   electronic ISSN 1554-6306   ISBN 978-0-4709-0295-0

The ASHE Higher Education Report is part of the Jossey-Bass Higher and Adult Education Series and is published six times a year by Wiley Subscription Services, Inc., A Wiley Company, at Jossey-Bass, 989 Market Street, San Francisco, California 94103-1741.

For subscription information, see the Back Issue/Subscription Order Form in the back of this volume.

CALL FOR PROPOSALS: Prospective authors are strongly encouraged to contact Kelly Ward (kaward@wsu.edu) or Lisa Wolf-Wendel (lwolf@ku.edu). See "About the ASHE Higher Education Report Series" in the back of this volume.

Visit the Jossey-Bass Web site at **www.josseybass.com.**

The ASHE Higher Education Report is indexed in CIJE: Current Index to Journals in Education (ERIC), Current Abstracts (EBSCO), Education Index/Abstracts (H.W. Wilson), ERIC Database (Education Resources Information Center), Higher Education Abstracts (Claremont Graduate University), IBR & IBZ: International Bibliographies of Periodical Literature (K.G. Saur), and Resources in Education (ERIC).

Advisory Board

The ASHE Higher Education Report Series is sponsored by the Association for the Study of Higher Education (ASHE), which provides an editorial advisory board of ASHE members.

Contents

Executive Summary

Partnerships and collaborations provide an opportunity to solve challenging issues facing higher education by parleying resources, knowledge, and skills of individual partners to achieve joint goals and objectives. Policymakers and funding agencies increasingly emphasize the need to partner, but merely dictating that partners work together does not predict success. Thus, although a demand exists for colleges and universities to engage in collaborations, more attention needs to be devoted regarding best practices for success.

Partnerships involve organizational-level joint ventures that may go by any number of names (strategic alliances, joint ventures, collaborations, partnerships). These initiatives can take several forms: between or among institutions, through departmental alliances across institutions, with university programs that pair with businesses or community agencies. Faculty pairings across institutions typically are referred to as collaborations rather than partnerships, although organizational partnerships may emerge from these initial faculty collaborations. Central to organizational or individual collaborations are a series of processes. Better understanding of how collaborations develop can thus result in more effective joint ventures.

Collaborations can come from a variety of motivations. Educational partnerships are formed for a range of reasons: to effect educational reform, provide regional economic development, allow dual enrollment for K–12 students, encourage transfer between community colleges and four-year universities, improve student learning, save on resources, obtain a shared goal or vision, and create international partnerships. It is important to understand more about partnerships to discern the reasons for their frequent failures and to highlight the structures and processes that promote success and sustainability. Partnerships have an impact on an organizational level, requiring layers of administrative oversight, new policies for the new partnership, and commitment of resources. Likewise, they have repercussions for faculty work, as faculty members often serve as initiators—champions—of collaboration.

A key tenet of partnering is that benefits accrue from creating a collaboration: individual partners cannot accomplish their overarching goals on their own, but a partnership creates the ultimate win-win situation. The failure of so many partnerships, however, raises concerns about how these joint ventures can succeed in the long term. As institutions enter into partnerships and policymakers contemplate mandates to encourage joint ventures, it is important to know what best supports partnering, what contributes to challenges that emerge in collaborations, and how to obtain long-term success.

The goal of this volume is to provide faculty and college leaders with an overview regarding formation of partnerships and to highlight elements of consideration for those contemplating a collaborative venture. As state coffers become depleted, policymakers must make choices in revenue spending and look at tactics to save state resources. Institutions of higher education are being challenged to change historical patterns of operation and to explore partnerships as a means of avoiding duplicate services, providing creative solutions for the problems facing colleges, and becoming more accountable. Partnerships affect college operations at different levels and in different ways throughout the institution; they do not operate in a vacuum.

The organizational context of each institution contributes to alignment of the partnership, with this overall context juxtaposed with the mission and structure of each involved institution. Other contributing contextual factors include the partners' need and desire to leverage resources, the role of the champion who believes in the cause, and the ease with which actions and decisions can take place. During initial formation, it is important to create a shared understanding of the problem. It is critical to create shared language to define the problem and the goals of the partnership.

Partnerships range from informal ventures to more formal affairs with operating procedures and governance systems. The antecedents that preface the creation of a partnership matter. The history of the partners' relationships cast a shadow on the current relationships, often making it easier for partners to work together because they are familiar with one another's work or because they have developed a shared understanding of the issue that they are working to address. Collaborations involve a dance of numerous partners, some of whom are driven to participate given their internal desire to cooperate, others who are told by superiors to participate or required by regulations. This mixture of motivations influences the course of the partnership over time.

Individual champions for partnerships bring different levels of social capital to the venture. Social capital represents the interconnections individuals have with one another and between social networks. The more connections a person has and the more access to critical resources, the more leverage available to move the partnership forward. Organizational capital, on the other hand, is thought of as a tangible resource. In this case, the capital might be space, technology, funding for materials, access to knowledge, or people. Access to organizational capital depends on the champion's centrality in an organization (Granovetter, 1983) and the density of relationships to leverage access to resources (Coleman, 1988).

A third factor impacting ventures involves the creation of partnership capital. In this instance, partnership capital forms when partners have created a sense of shared meaning about their activities together and a shared network develops. When individual partners move past individual interests to common goals and mission, partnership capital forms. It is the strength of social networks that fosters the development of social capital among partners in these collaborations. Through the formation of partnership capital, a capacity is created that could not be obtained alone or by the mere sharing of resources. Over time, shared norms are formed among partners as a result of negotiation, time together to build trust, and formation of shared knowledge and meaning for ideas and visions regarding the joint venture. In the process of institutionalizing the partnership, it moves beyond the individual partners and organizations and becomes a different construct—partnership capital.

Collaborations also occur outside the confines of institutional involvement, primarily in traditional forms of faculty members' working together. It is often in this individual work, however, that collaborations have their roots. As a result of this genesis of partnerships from initial work by individual faculty, it is important to understand the roles of original collaborators and how these links may progress to form institutional partnerships. Faculty champions serve a critical role in the formation of partnerships. They are able to provide the ground-level work required to bring partners together and can use their influence in their home institutions to obtain commitment of organizational capital. Academic leaders must recognize these important contributions and work them into the reward system by adjusting policy to recognize these efforts. Creating incubator spaces for these initiatives to operate—and space to fail—is important.

International partnerships add another layer to the formation and development of partnerships. The expansion of the global marketplace and opening of borders formerly closed to the United States provide a number of opportunities for partnering. Nevertheless, recent research reports that U.S. faculty members are less involved with international efforts (Finkelstein, Walker, and Chen, 2009). As with domestic partnerships, several key features contribute to successful joint ventures. Heffernan and Poole (2005) found that clear communication of expectations, trust generated by time spent working together and understanding partners' strengths, and obvious commitment to the project were critical to a partnership's viability. It is important to pay attention to the detailed work of the collaboration, including agreements on funding disbursements and obligations, contractual obligations such as the timing of academic calendars and course delivery, and common understanding of underlying value systems that are rooted in cultural differences (Tedrow and Mabokela, 2007).

Understanding the challenges facing colleges and universities is the first step in establishing a partnership (Davies, 2006). Environmental scanning involves gathering various forms of data to analyze and determine the best strategic tactics available. Colleges and universities have borrowed from business practices (Birnbaum, 2000) such as S-W-O-T analyses to outline strengths, weaknesses, opportunities, and threats and P-E-S-T analyses to consider political, economical, social, and technological contexts. Strategic collaborations are needed in the future. Strategic partnerships differ from the unplanned collaborations of the past: they are entered into to meet institutional strategic goals and to build institutional capacity (Zeelen and van der Linden, 2009).

Key to a partnership's success is building relationships (Baus and Rams-bottom, 1999; Heffernan and Poole, 2005). Relationships are first built between individuals and then shift to institutions. Central to these efforts is the role of a champion to jump-start the joint effort. Next, open communication helps to build trust to help maintain momentum. Burgeoning relationships help to solidify commitment to the joint venture and help to create a shared vision for the group, resulting in buy-in from the various parties involved. Likewise, support from positional leaders provides additional motivation for partners, as the venture is valued in the organization. The framing of the partnership for stakeholders and partners helps bond those in the collaboration to a common understanding of what it means. Thus, sense making is a critical component of long-term success.

Partnerships become increasingly important as challenges build for institutions of higher education. Colleges and universities must select from an array of opportunities. Faculty collaborators, institutional leaders, and policymakers all need to ask questions and reflect on their own motivations to collaborate before entering joint ventures. First, assessing motivations to partner will address what resources are available and what individual objectives are. Second, the importance of relationships in partnering is well documented. Thus, it is critical to devote the time required to foster relationships and to allow time to build trust among partners. Third, aligning rewards and governance structures must be ensured to value collaborative efforts. Finally, partnerships based on shared visions or goals create a synergy and buy-in for participants that help cement relationships and build trust in seeking common desires.

In sum, key supports to develop and sustain strategic partnerships include strong relationships nurtured over time, trust, frequent and open communication, shared values and vision, and a common understanding of what it means to be involved in the partnership. Constant evaluation of the collaborative efforts helps inform those involved so that adjustments can be made. The creation of a governance process creates the framework required to support the partnership and the policies that oversee the ways in which feedback is obtained and future plans made. The challenges facing higher education require rethinking and reconceptualizing business as usual. Partnerships provide an answer for some of these challenges.

Foreword

Throughout history, higher education has had to be creative in how it addressed access and opportunity, delivered educational services, and made the most of available resources. The first decade of the new millennium has not been an exception. With calls for accountability, innovation, and expanding access coupled with significant economic recession and increased public skepticism about institutions' ability to deliver effective and efficient educational experiences for increasingly diverse learners, the future looks no less demanding. Given the cacophony of reports, federal and state directives, and foundation and association initiatives that touch on almost every aspect of higher education (the Spellings Commission, the American Graduation Initiative, Race to the Top, Liberal Education, and America's Promise, for example), it is not surprising that campus leaders and faculty are trying to build capacity that will better address growing internal and external demands on postsecondary systems. One form of capacity building is collaborations or partnerships.

Collaborations are not new to higher education. We have long acknowledged the importance of team teaching, research teams, and student guidance committees, while task forces and committees of every kind are the typical response to information gathering, institutional assessments, and faculty governance at all levels. As embedded in the higher education system as forms of coordination may be, we have seen far less focus on understanding how these configurations are generated, how to help them work effectively, and how to sustain them, especially if original funding or support expires. Even more absent is consideration of how such arrangements are strategically cultivated as the means through which critical challenges and concerns facing higher education could be addressed. Presidents, deans, department chairs, and faculty leaders are often left with a handful of sources spanning the last twenty years that provide pieces of the larger puzzle or perspectives targeting quite specific agendas.

In this monograph, Pamela Eddy compiles a comprehensive review of the extant higher education literature about forms of collaborations and partnerships. Her critical examination lays out the rationale and impetus for collaboration, identifying factors underlying the conditions that promote the need for partnerships as well those that make these efforts challenging. Eddy considers partnerships from three vantage points. The first, an organizational perspective, provides insights for senior leaders who need to consider mission alignment, strategy, resource distribution, systems, and legal issues and to create environments in which others can initiate innovative relationships. Eddy then focuses on individual partnerships such as faculty collaborations about which we may be more aware through dual appointments of faculty, interdisciplinary academic units, and joint research proposals. She explores the importance of faculty investment, the role of champions in successful partnerships, and issues of sustainability when interests (and resources) shift or when it is time to embed the initiative into institutional culture. Finally, Eddy examines collaboration through a futures lens, considering ways in which partnerships provide simultaneously facile and stable foundations for innovation, global cooperation, technological advancement, and capacity building. The inclusion of international partnership examples in this section is particularly unique in reviews of this kind. Eddy ends with a model of strategic partnerships emanating from factors contributing to the successful collaborations she outlines.

This monograph looks at key aspects of partnerships: methods of forming them; cultivating interest in and commitment to them; appropriate processes depending on the cultures of organizations, involvement, and leadership; leveraging the capital and resources of each partner and realizing these changes over time; intellectual capital and knowledge production as both means and ends. The examples used throughout to illustrate these factors across the three perspectives help senior leaders, administrators, faculty, and policymakers understand how educational units and organizations can work together more closely to achieve mutually beneficial ends while cultivating trusting and deeper relationships on which to build future collaborations.

Marilyn Amey
Professor of Higher Education at
Michigan State University

Acknowledgments

Previous work on partnerships and collaborations paved the pathway for how I began to think about writing about the current status of research in this area. Not only did the early work by Ann Austin and Roger Baldwin (1991) regarding faculty as collaborators provide a foundation for this book's section on individual level collaborations, it also influences how I approach joint ventures with others. Both Ann and Roger model what it means to be part of an effective team, and I use their example when I work with others.

I have been working with Marilyn Amey and other collaborators for the past five years to explore various aspects of partnerships. These ongoing conversations and projects contributed to this work and my thinking. This current work would not be possible without the base upon which it was built via this previous research. In my writing, I found myself conscious of our ongoing dialogue and as a result attentive to these collaborators as an audience for this work and as an integral part of my thought process when writing.

Finally, I would like to acknowledge the time my family has devoted to supporting my research efforts. My husband, David Pape, created space for me to work on this book by taking over numerous responsibilities in keeping our household running. My children, Andrew, Jeffrey, and Laura, grew accustomed to my conversations with them about collaborations as they faced their school projects and provided feedback on the various models I was creating for this work. Without the support of my family, this writing would have been impossible to complete. They are the important collaborators in this research.

Published online in Wiley InterScience
(www.interscience.wiley.com) • DOI: 10.1002/aehe.3602

Overview

PARTNERSHIPS AND COLLABORATIONS are advocated as a means to address problems plaguing higher education. Partnerships involve organizational joint ventures that may go by any number of names (strategic alliances, joint ventures, collaborations, partnerships, to name a few). These initiatives can take several forms—between or among institutions, through departmental alliances across institutions, or with university programs that pair with businesses or community agencies. Faculty pairings across institutions typically are referred to as collaborations rather than partnerships, though from these initial faculty collaborations, organizational partnerships may emerge. Central to organizational or individual collaborations are a series of processes. Better understanding of the components of how collaborations develop can thus result in more effective joint ventures.

Why is it important to know more about partnerships and collaborations? State policymakers want to avoid redundant efforts and duplicate state spending in education (Van de Water and Rainwater, 2001) and often look to P–16 collaborations to streamline educational pathways for students (Leskes, 2006; Yff, 1996) as one method to create efficiencies. Institutions favor partnerships as a means to leverage resources and pool talent as they tackle challenging issues (Russell and Flynn, 2000). Individuals value partnerships because they allow for professional collaboration, in particular when they are members of academic units in which they are the only specialist in a disciplinary area (Creamer, 2004). Institutions of higher education often serve as brokers in partnerships (Amey, Eddy, and Ozaki, 2007). Maimon (2006) posits that the university should be viewed as a public square that creates the ideal place for sharing and a common place where partnerships can develop. Thus, colleges provide a fertile ground for creating a range of collaborative efforts. Although multiple reasons exist for creating partnerships, these collaborations often fail (Eddy, 2007; Farrell and Seifert, 2007).

It is important to understand more about partnerships to discern the reasons for their frequent failures and to highlight the structures and processes that promote success and sustainability. Partnerships have an impact on an organizational level, requiring layers of administrative oversight, creation of policies for the new partnership, and a commitment of resources. Likewise, faculty work has repercussions as faculty members get involved in these collaborations and often serve as the initiator of the collaboration in the role of champion. The shifting nature of faculty work (Gappa, Austin, and Trice, 2007) calls for interdisciplinary teaching to support student learning (Holley, 2009) and requires faculty to collaborate in new and different ways. What remains unknown is how faculty are rewarded for their participation in partnerships and what effect this participation has on achieving the various goals outlined for the collaboration.

A key tenet of partnering is that a benefit comes from creating a collaboration based on the ideal that the individual partners cannot accomplish their goals on their own: the partnership creates the ultimate win-win situation. But partnerships are not always successful (Reed, Cooper, and Young, 2007), even when mandated by state policy (Farrell and Seifert, 2007). As institutions enter into partnerships and policymakers contemplate mandates to encourage joint ventures, it is important to know what best supports partnering, what contributes to challenges that emerge in collaborations, and how to obtain long-term success.

A variety of reasons exist that motivate individuals and institutions to create partnerships. Lefever-Davis, Johnson, and Pearman (2007) note the need to recognize that partners exist in distinctive milieus where roles and expectations differ. Past relationships, shared goals, and forms of communication all contribute to the formation of partnerships. These antecedent rationales for partnering affect how the partnership is formed and create expectations of the partners regarding their roles in the partnership. Ultimately, success and sustainability of the collaboration have their roots in the initial context of the formation of the partnerships.

Despite the pitfalls of partnering, the push is present for creating joint ventures. External demands on institutions of higher education and shifts in college structures and faculty expectations resulting from collaborative efforts also raise a number of questions: How are partnerships formed? What are best practices from institutions involved in successful and sustainable partnerships? How do different institutional cultures affect partnerships, in particular when these partnerships are global? What shifts in faculty rewards are required to recognize and support faculty collaboration with a partnership? What type of practices best support joint faculty work? Seven themes help define the various motivations for creating partnerships in practice: (1) educational reform, (2) economic development, (3) dual enrollment or student transfer, (4) student learning, (5) resource savings, (6) shared goals and visions, and (7) international joint ventures. Examples in each section provide the foundation for a more thorough understanding of what goes into the formation and development of partnerships. Even though these themes are presented as distinct rationales and goals for collaborations, partnerships by their nature are messy and complex; thus, multiple motivators may be operating in a partnership. Generally, however, a dominant rationale exists for partnering that contributes to the culture of the relationship. The following section explicates the seven types of partnership rationales and provides working concepts to aid the reader as they approach the rest of the volume.

Motivating Factors for Partnerships and Collaborations

Joint ventures are often referred to as partnerships, alliances, or collaborations, but these ventures vary in motivations for members to join, rationales for cooperating, and ability to sustain. As well, who is involved and the objectives of the pairing influence the definitions of the collaboration. For the purposes of this volume, partnerships refer to organizational pairings that may range from the informal to the more formal. These collaborations involve a college or university unit's working with another unit collaborator at a different institution or with businesses or community agencies. Individual faculty working together, on the other hand, are referred to as collaborators rather than partners.

Educational partnerships are formed for a variety of reasons: to effect educational reform, to provide regional economic development, to allow dual enrollment for K–12 students, to encourage transfer between community colleges and four-year universities, to improve student learning, to save on resources, to obtain a shared goal or vision, to create international partnerships. Each partnership employs definitions of partnership or collaboration that suit its distinct context and group goals that may result in a lack of shared meaning when use of similar terms in fact carries different meanings for those involved. Clifford and Millar (2008) determined in their review of the K–16 partnership literature that current research contains gaps in how partnerships are formed and maintained and that partnership is not defined. To help address this shortcoming, the following section reviews the various motivations guiding the development of partnerships based on the focal point in the partnering goals. Nuances in the definition of partnership or collaboration are apparent in how the overarching objectives of the partnership frame and define the language used to describe the group process.

Educational Reform

Reports such as *A Nation at Risk* (National Commission on Excellence in Education, 1983) and the Spellings Report (U.S. Department of Education, 2006) have pointed to the need to change educational systems and the need for systemic change in educational systems (Hirota, 2005; Maeroff, Callan, and Usdan, 2001). Reform requires new ways of thinking about roles and methods for change (Fullan, 2002). For example, reform efforts seek to redress educational systems that do not support historically underrepresented minorities (Baxter, 2008) and to hold educational systems accountable for student learning (see, for example, the No Child Left Behind Act of 2001 [P.L. 107–10] and the Spellings Report [U.S. Department of Education, 2006]). At the core of educational reform are the beliefs that current systems are ineffective in obtaining desired levels of student outcomes and partnerships provide a means to achieve these goals.

Furthermore, the increase in for-profit educational providers changes the landscape of higher education, as these institutions provide an alternative for students and a means to address educational reform. The advent of for-profits increases competition in higher education. Existing institutions of higher education often partner together to provide a larger array of services to compete with the more service-oriented and focused missions of the for-profits (Shapiro, 2002).

One reform effort taking root and driving partnerships is the notion of a seamless educational system. The intention of the creation of a P–16 pipeline is based on the belief that the pipeline requires commonality of goals to educate students across the educational continuum (Rochford, O'Neill, Gelb, and Ross, 2005, 2007). Several states have initiated P–16 initiatives that vary from mandated programs to voluntary task forces (Yff, 1996), but legislators face numerous issues each year and can address only a select few (Fowler, 2009). Thus, a lack of a continuous focus on P–16 initiatives often results in such partnerships faltering. In 2009, the American Association of State Colleges and Universities identified college readiness as one of the top ten policy issues facing states and concluded that a key strategy in addressing this issue was collaborations developed through P–16 initiatives.

Economic Development

Partnerships are seen as means of enhancing economic development. Federal funding agencies such as the National Science Foundation look to support partnerships that allow for technology transfer between colleges and business to help support economic development. Another form of partnerships with a goal of economic development centers on workforce development plans. Kearney and others (2007) studied a multiyear university-government partnership concerning workforce development and found that the collaboration helped align training to employers' needs more closely. The findings underscore the need to understand the context and industry mission of workforce education programs.

Key to partnerships with a goal of economic development is identifying and fostering a mutual benefit (Kruss, 2006) that moves beyond traditional forms of consultancy toward a more strategic approach of planning and operations with an eye toward long-term sustainability. Partnerships built on trust, communication, and common purposes are more successful, whereas inequality among the partners and fewer resources undermine joint ventures (Connolly, Jones, and Jones, 2007).

An international example is Queensland University of Technology's partnering with the city of Brisbane and the state of Queensland to stimulate what they call "creative industry" that melded together brick-and-mortar initiatives and programming (Silka, 2008). Economic development initiatives often entail regional efforts to address issues or challenges facing multiple organizations (Fluharty, 2007). As the global economy reels from economic recession, partnerships are increasingly looked upon as a viable lever for economic recovery and development (Dominguez, 2006).

Dual Enrollment or Student Transfer

Two key transition points involving different educational partnerships occur at the nexus of high school and college (dual enrollment) and between community colleges and four-year universities (transfer). Dual enrollment and transfer require partnering among K–12 schools, community colleges, and universities that is often legislatively mandated. Dual enrollment occurs when high-ability high school students enroll concurrently in an institution of higher education, typically a community college, to help meet their educational needs for more advanced coursework (Kreuger, 2006; Morrison, 2008). Currently, forty-seven states have dual enrollment programs in place (Farrell and Seifert, 2007). States vary in oversight of these programs, from state statutes to board policies to institutional policies. States differ as well on who is responsible for payment of dual-enrollment coursework and how high school and college credits are awarded (Hale, 2001).

College transfer occurs when students move between a community college and four-year college or between two four-year institutions. Kisker (2005) determined key elements in community college transfer included previous relationships between institutions, the support of the college presidents, adequate and sustained funding, and the importance of the university in maintaining a presence on the community college campus. Typically, articulation agreements between community colleges and universities outline the requirements of the transfer process, potentially eliminating common barriers and challenges faced in partnerships development (see, for example Anderson and Sundre, 2005). Ease of movement between educational institutions helps in retaining students, eliminates redundancy in course taking, and may result in cost savings for students and their families.

Student Learning

Institutions are often motivated to partner because they share interest in students' success. One focus of student learning initiatives involves preparing students for college. These collaborations often target underserved groups through programs such as TRIO, Upward Bound, and locally created access programs (Hebel, 2007; Lindstrom and others, 2009). These programs involve colleges' and universities' partnering with public schools and community groups to open paths to college for students not typically attending. Another focus of partnership centered on student learning involves service learning. Despite challenges in building and sustaining service-learning collaborations, Sandy and Holland (2006) discovered a high sense of understanding and commitment to student learning among partners, with the common goal of student learning helping to bolster the partnerships. Another focus on student learning occurs in vocational training programs in community colleges that work to support apprenticeships for students in area businesses (Chin, Bell, Munby, and Hutchinson, 2004: Cohen and Brawer, 2008) and in technology preparation programs that provide high school students with work experiences (Bragg, 2000).

As noted earlier, a common area of partnership activity occurs among educational institutions along the P–16 continuum (Kisker and Hauser, 2007; Tafel and Eberhart, 1999). P–16 initiatives not only address educational reform but also offer opportunities to partner to heighten student learning. Though the overarching goal of all educational institutions is to educate students, differences in culture, teaching approaches, policy oversight, and philosophies emerge (Krueger, 2006; Zimpher, 2002). For example, Bartholomew and Sandholtz (2009) reviewed a partnership between a school and a university, noting that different views on the teacher's role in school reform created fissures in the partnership. Different perspectives ultimately shifted the goals and outcomes of the collaboration.

Resource Savings

The decline in public funding for higher education pushes faculty and institutions to seek supplementary revenue sources and to look at partnerships as a money-saving enterprise (Daniel, 2002). For example, educational institutions involved in P–16 endeavors can help states save resources but require a reduction in the competitive nature of higher education (Baker, 2002). Resource savings are often a motivator for institutions in rural areas that strive to create better opportunities for students, businesses, and the community (Warren and Peel, 2005). Although one source of revenue comes from partnering with business, an issue often raised in business and educational partnerships is the loss of academic freedom for faculty members and the push of a business agenda (Slaughter and Rhoades, 2004). Concerns also occur regarding the impact on the academic culture, but Mendoza and Berger (2008) found that the faculty in the case investigated felt that the academic culture of their department was unaffected by their partnership with industry collaborators. Kisker and Carducci (2003) provided a different perspective on education-business partnerships, underscoring the symbiotic relationships between regional employers and community college programs. In this case, businesses receive a well-trained workforce, colleges create cutting-edge curricula to support student learning, and students gain valued experience in the workforce.

Federal grant funding agencies encourage partnerships between public schools and colleges as a means to pool resources and address problems of poor student performance (Clifford and Millar, 2008). A common perception is that alliances result in economies of scale and ultimately the expenditure of fewer resources. One form of resource savings occurs when partners share facilities (McCord, 2002). Watson (2007) studied a partnership among a high school, community college, and four-year university in which the construction of a new high school afforded the opportunity to create space to include programs on site provided by the two-year college and the four-year university. Each educational representative held different motivations and desires for sharing space, but all were accommodated in the high school space.

Shared Goals and Visions

Another motivation for partnering is based on partners' having common desires for particular outcomes. Having a shared goal or vision for a partnership may be based on a number of factors, including those motivations outlined above. An example of shared goals occurring on a policy level involved the Association of Research Libraries and the Association of American

Universities. ARL Executive Director Duane Webster was a champion of the partnership that benefited both associations but more so of those that were part of a larger set of partnerships and collaborations (Vaughn, 2009). Another example of an informal partnership between associations involves the sharing of student data in New Hampshire for policymakers regarding postsecondary aspirations of students across the state (Lemaire, Knapp, and Lowe, 2008). Here the goal of pooling information using a collaborative helped address the lack of consistent data on higher education in the state, ultimately providing a benefit for all institutions and students.

As partnerships become more frequent, state offices create policies to outline how agreements should be operationalized and to help support new partners in defining roles and responsibilities (Illinois State Department of Human Resources, 2001). Likewise, colleges partner with community agencies to obtain shared goals and desirable outcomes such as improved health and safety, community betterment, or common desires to enhance learning opportunities. The closer the alignment of the shared vision, the more likely the partnership will become sustainable and reach its goals (Kruss, 2006).

International Joint Ventures

Colleges and universities increasingly look across national borders to establish international partnerships. Efficiencies in communications and travel and the opening of previously closed countries like China have created possibilities for cross-border projects. The need for creating new educational markets to supplement college resources and provide educational opportunities to support students in acquiring global competencies and reliance on the knowledge industry (McMurtrie and Wheeler, 2008) all provide motivation for working with foreign counties. Traditionally, study abroad or individual faculty collaborations with scholars around the world formed the backbone of international efforts (Eggins, 2003). U.S. faculty, however, have lagged in their involvement in international research or teaching relative to faculty in other countries (Finkelstein, Walker, and Chen, 2009; O'Hara, 2009).

International partnerships are more complex because of the additional considerations resulting from use of different languages and working in different cultures (Scarino, Crichton, and Woods, 2007). The policies of each country's government and the colleges and universities involved "play a crucial role in determining the nature of foreign study opportunities and in shaping the realities of the experience" (Altbach, 1998, p. 151). How these national policies translate to operations for faculty and colleges contributes to a successful partnership. For instance, the Bologna process was developed across countries in Europe but has real implications for those managing course credit transfers for students and for faculty coordination regarding curriculum. According to de Wit (2002), "Strategic partnerships in research, teaching, and transfer of knowledge, between universities and of universities with business and beyond national borders, will be the future for higher education in order to manage the challenges that globalization will place on it" (p. 205). Knowing more about the partnership process will aid faculty, leaders, and policymakers in creating sustainable joint ventures.

Looking Forward

A broad definition of partnership is used in this volume to accommodate the range of partnering options, motivations, and outcomes. Partnerships are considered a collaborative between two or more institutions of higher education, businesses, or social agencies, with the goal of obtaining a shared objective. As noted, the ultimate objective may range from resource saving to economic development to increased student learning outcomes. Regardless of the desired end product, it is critical for those entering into a partnership to have a clearly defined notion of the partnership. For the purposes of this monograph, a partnership involves two or more organizations working together to obtain an agreed-upon objective, whereas collaboration describes instances of individual faculty working together.

This volume comprises three chapters. The next chapter reviews organizational partnerships. The rationale for organizations and individuals to participate in institutional collaborations sets the foundation for the development of the partnership, builds on preconceived ideas regarding roles in the group and the level of resources each contributes to the project, and begins to define the type and level of connections each participant brings to the group. The preliminary phases of a partnership rely on the various levels of social capital that individual actors bring to the endeavor as well as the type of organizational capital committed to the project. Amey, Eddy, Campbell, and Watson (2008) found that a new form of capital develops in collaborations, namely *partnership capital*. Partnership capital evolves over time as group members develop trust of one another; build shared meaning and understanding about ideas, goals, and outcomes associated with the partnership; and solidify the network of those involved in such a manner that the partnership can outlive those immediately involved.

The second chapter addresses individual faculty collaborations and roles. Two levels of practice are evident in the individual sphere. First is the role of the individual champion in an organizational collaboration. As noted in the previous chapter, individuals bring different levels of social capital to the exchange, and often a person takes on the role of champion of the project. The chapter discusses the role of the champion, paying attention to issues of sustainability and succession of leaders. According to Zakocs, Tiwari, Vehige, and DeJong (2008), the role of the champion is critical to success of the partnership. These authors investigated a series of five community-university partnerships and determined three key factors supported success: (1) designation of a college staff member to act as a community facilitator; (2) support from higher-level college administrators; and (3) community initiation of the partnership. In this research, the presence of a dedicated individual supported the partnership. The second level of practice reviews collaborations based on various forms of group work in which faculty members participate. Here, the faculty collaboration may be focused on research, teaching, or practice.

Faculty members often serve as the initial instigators for partnerships that grow among organizations (Amey, 2010; Cooper and Mitsunaga, 2010). The focus on the roles of faculty, however, does not include faculty collaborations in a single institution such as those involved in interdisciplinary work (Holley, 2009; Lattuca, 2001) or faculty work on joint research projects for publication (Austin and Baldwin, 1991). This chapter reviews the roles the faculty play in these early stages of collaborative ventures. It also includes an overview of the role of the champion in the collaboration. In this case, the champion may or may not be the initial faculty member involved in the partnership.

The final chapter posits the role of collaborative work in future endeavors where institutions of higher education are involved. In contemplating the future and potential partnerships, it is important for leaders to consider expectations of their institutional roles, barriers to successful partnering outcomes, and best practices to support successful collaboration. This chapter reviews the role of goals on partnership outcomes, the demands of international partnerships, and tips on planning for partnerships.

The recent explosion of international partnering opportunities is reviewed from the vantage point of the U.S. partner (Fischer, 2009). Internationally, more countries are increasing their investment in higher education (Labi, 2009a, 2009b), just at the time when U.S. institutions of higher education are receiving less support through state appropriations. Coupled with increased international investment in postsecondary universities is the desire to create *world-class* institutions (Hazelkorn, 2009). To that end, U.S. institutions are under pressure to keep up with a larger array of competitors for prestige and to stave off the slip in international rankings of top universities (Huckabee, 2008).

Foreign countries seek to partner with U.S. colleges but are selective regarding these partnerships. For instance, China is becoming more discriminating regarding its institutional partners, demanding more commitment from U.S. partners and focusing on longer-term partnerships (Willis, 2006). Likewise, U.S. colleges are challenged in their partnering with overseas institutions (Mooney, 2008) as a result of differences in expectations, culture, and measures of quality.

The goal of this volume is to provide faculty and college leaders with an overview regarding formation of partnerships and to highlight elements of consideration for those contemplating a collaborative venture. Faculty members will be able to take into account how their involvement in a partnership is valued in the tenure and promotion cycle and to determine how to anticipate potential problems arising from collaborative efforts. A thorough review of interdisciplinary work (Holley, 2009) addresses faculty roles and institutional actions regarding this particular form of internal institutional collaboration but is not included in this volume. Rather, the faculty roles included cover involvement in partnerships across institutions that go beyond mere collaboration on a research project, though these types of pairings may ultimately provide the foundation for larger institutional collaborations. College leaders will learn what factors are central to establishing sustainable partnerships, what barriers exist to partnership formation and success, and how to think of partnerships more strategically. Leaders will also discover ways to support the faculty work that is often the backbone of joint ventures.

The objectives of this volume include an outline of the features of partnerships to enhance understanding of the component parts of these ventures. The information presented provides individuals and institutions tools to analyze joint ventures before committing to a partnership and outlines tactics used in successful collaborations as well as challenges to their sustainability. Finally, it provides suggestions that focus on a number of different levels of involvement to help leverage successful partnering.

The audience for this volume includes individuals active in partnerships or interested in starting a joint collaboration. College, business, and community leaders will find this volume useful as they pursue joint ventures. In particular, it is important to ask a set of questions up front as partnerships are created. The impetus for partnerships often begins with a champion of the project; thus, knowing more about this critical role can help leverage the processes involved in collaborating. Institutional leaders are barraged with opportunities to partner with others. The information presented here helps leaders understand better which partnerships are more advantageous, what stages are most critical for long-term success, and how best to use institutional resources in the partnerships. Finally, policymakers and funding agencies increasingly emphasize partnerships as a means to advance state, national, and disciplinary goals (Chamberlin and Plucker, 2008; Frierson-Campbell, 2003). Tracking data along the educational pipeline requires collaboration among institutions (Olson, 2006). Thus, knowing more about what contributes to a successful partnership can help shape how mandates are crafted and grant language formed to best support successful partnerships.

Current trends in higher education point to an increased demand for partnerships, often with the expressed desire to save resources. Perceived duplication of services in an institution and among colleges and universities in a state push policymakers to create mandates requiring cooperation. A common form of these mandates is P–16 initiatives to create a seamless educational path among educational sectors, with transition points between public schools and colleges and between two-year colleges and four-year colleges. Leskes (2006) researched an initiative focused on college access and noted that long-term success required becoming more intentional in aligning actions with desired outcomes. Work on seamless educational systems builds on the ideas of ways to best support student learning and potential, thus underscoring the need for alignment. Further, a report by the task force on urban and metropolitan schools for the American Association of State Colleges and Universities (2004) determined that personnel need to be able to move easily back and forth across the boundary of P–12 and higher education and act as boundary spanners. These individuals can act as champions in the collaborative process and highlight how alliances benefit from these porous configurations.

As state coffers become depleted, policymakers must choose how to spend scarce resources and look at tactics to save them. Increasingly, institutional mergers are also advocated as a means to save state resources (Blumenstyk, 2009; Harmon and Harmon, 2008). Likewise, grant-funding agencies are also interested in economies of scale, desiring to have the most impact for their funds. Collaborations are increasingly a part of calls for proposals.

More and more case study research in the field is beginning to be reported about partnerships (see, for example, Amey, 2007; Holland, 2010). This work helps to fill in the gaps of our knowledge about partnerships and provides others with templates and models based on successful ventures. Examples of partnerships that did not work are equally important, as they identify potential barriers and pitfalls to avoid.

Implications for Higher Education

Institutions of higher education are being challenged to shift out of historical patterns of operation and to explore partnerships as efficient means of avoiding duplicate services, providing creative solutions for the problems facing colleges, and becoming more accountable. Past practice shows, however, that mandating collaboration is no guarantee of success (Farrell and Seifert, 2007). Partnerships affect college operations at different levels and in different ways throughout the institution. Policymakers can structure mandates for collaboration more effectively when they understand more fully what best supports the formation of partnerships and their development and what helps maintain longer-term sustainability. Institutional leaders must weigh options as they consider what partnerships are most beneficial for their colleges, the best way to expend scarce college resources, and how to support faculty members' engaging in partnerships. Likewise, faculty members act in leadership roles when they serve as early champions of partnerships.

Given the fact that partnerships are initiated by different individuals throughout the college, leadership's responses likewise occur throughout the institution—starting with the department chair and moving up the organizational hierarchy to the president. Leadership decisions are different and represent various levels of college commitment, depending on the stage where these decisions are made. Individual faculty and staff can leverage their interactions on the front line more effectively when they understand better the systematic impact of the interactions involved in partnerships. Individuals often serve as the initial champions for partnerships, working at the grass-roots level with their personal connections and involvement in particular areas of interest. Thus, faculty members need to determine how their involvement in partnerships is recognized in the current reward structure, in particular if they serve as the initial champion for the partnership because that role typically requires more time and energy than just participation in an established partnership. A heightened awareness of their own power and capital allows champions the ability to leverage change to best support the development of a partnership. Knowing more about partnership operations, in particular the effective levers for change, can help college leaders and champions prepare more effectively for the future.

Organizational Partnerships

A S NOTED, PARTNERSHIPS AND COLLABORATIONS occur on a number of different levels. This chapter reviews issues relative to the organizational structures of the partnering institutions and the interactions relevant to formation and development of partnerships. This macroperspective looks at institutional reasons for seeking out partnerships and deconstructs key features of collaborating from an organizational vantage point. Central to the creation of partnerships are the institutional motivations driving their initiation. Motivations emerge for partners based on the ultimate goals of the collaboration, with some being economically driven and others more altruistically oriented.

Partnerships do not operate in a vacuum. The organizational context of each organization contributes to alignment of the partnership, and this overall context is juxtaposed with the mission and structure of each involved institution. Other contributing contextual factors include the partners' need and desire to leverage resources, the role of the champion who believes in the cause, and the ease with which actions and decisions can take place.

This chapter consists of four sections: the formation of partnerships, social capital, organizational capital, and partnership capital. First, it reviews in detail the elements involved in forming a partnership. Two main levers of influence contribute to the formation of partnerships—individual actions based on a person's accumulation of social capital and the resources that can be used in an organization such as assets, structures, and policies. Particular attention is given to the role of the champion in the development of the partnership. That role is viewed from an organizational level. The distinction on the individual level is that the joint venture does not occur for personal interests of research or goals, rather for larger institutional reasons. Finally, when partnerships move beyond merely situations of convenience and become true collaborative ventures, partnership capital forms. Partnership capital emerges as a result of the synergy of the constellation of partners and is able to operate without needing particular individuals involved—moving beyond the social capital of one or a few to capital generated from the group process itself.

Forming Partnerships

The reasons for forming a partnership are varied, with motivations being driven intrinsically or extrinsically or sometimes simultaneously. Likewise, the rationale or goals for creating a partnership often are rooted in these different types of motivation. For instance, if institutions are mandated to collaborate, partners may not bring much intrinsic motivation to the effort or high levels of trust for their collaborators. On the other hand, if a partnership forms based on mutual interests or shared goals, higher levels of intrinsic motivation are present and a different context exists for the partnership to operate.

The process of forming a partnership is iterative and does not necessarily occur in an orderly progression of linear steps. Yet some patterns emerge regarding the various stages of partnerships. Gray (1989) outlined three phases in the collaborative process: problem setting, direction setting, and implementation. The ways in which the collaboration is initially framed and the problems defined set the stage for the collaboration. An underlying element of defining the driving issue and creating a plan to address the concern is the role of leadership. In this case, a person or persons take on the champion role to help frame the core subject for others and to persuade stakeholders of the need to participate in and support the partnership.

The process of initial formation is reminiscent of Tuckman's model of team development (1965), which includes the stages of forming, storming, norming, and performing. In the initial stages of formation, it is important to create a shared understanding of the problem. Here, it is critical to create shared language to define the problem and the goals of the partnership (Bracken, 2007). Building trust (Johnston, 2009; Reyes, Alexander, and Diem, 2008) is a critical element in the storming phase when partners are just coming together. The initial seeds for building trust are rooted in the social capital that the champion brings to the endeavor. As the partnership takes root, new norms are established for how the group will work together. One outcome may be the institutionalization of the partnership, but, as noted, more often than not partnerships fail (Farrell and Seifert, 2007; Reed, Cooper, and Young, 2007).

To understand better the early stages of partnership formation, several areas are reviewed. First, it is important to understand the various forms that partnerships take on the range from informal pairings to more highly regulated formal collaborations. Next, the motivation factors that jump-start partnerships indicate different starting points for those involved. Finally, the context of organizational change provides a backdrop in which alliances form and showcases the influence of the change process on burgeoning partnerships. Throughout this formation phase, champions provide leadership and a source of influence in the process.

Forms of Partnerships

Partnerships range in the formality of their structure. Often, initial forays into partnering begin informally, a result of individuals' interest in working together, a desire to address a common problem, or the mere fact of being at the nexus at the right time and right place. Cooper and Mitsunaga (2010) report on the development of a series of international partnerships as a result of initial informal faculty work in foreign countries. Faculty members laid the foundation in their work for what later became more formal partnerships as represented by the creation of memorandums of understanding. Other types of informal collaborations include links initiated by school personnel and area businesses or with alumni and college foundation programs (Johnson, 2007).

According to Lattuca and Creamer (2005), "College and university faculty collaborate when they need to get things done" (p. 3). Reaching a shared goal is what drives these informal partnerships. In this case, no one has mandated that individuals or organizations work together; instead, they work collaboratively for different reasons. The informal nature of the alliances allows for ease of entry and exit from the pairings. This type of loose coupling (Weick, 1976) permits each partner to preserve its own identity and allows for the partnership to be dissolved. Loose coupling means that the partners are able to initiate localized adaptation, the partnership is inexpensive to operate, and partners are allowed space for self-determination. An example of an informal partnership reviewed by Krasnow (1997) reports on a collaboration among parents, teachers, and university researchers to develop and initiate a transition program from Head Start to kindergarten. In this case, a fragile cohesiveness existed, but it was tested by clashing paradigms of understanding and team needs and goals. This case highlights some of the difficulties present at the inception of informal partnerships. The lack of clear leadership also contributed to the demise of this alliance.

Another form of informal partnerships includes the formation of consortia among colleges. Baus and Ramsbottom (1999) reviewed definitions of academic consortia and compared them to those outlined by Patterson (1970). They outline a framework for consortia built on several criteria: they are voluntary, multi-institutional and not merely bilateral, multifunctional rather than single purpose, benefit from long-term member support, and are managed by a professional staff (p. 4). The connections that help keep such informal partnerships together are clear benefits attributable to the ventures and the support offered by paid staff. Even though the office staff members do not necessarily provide leadership, they do provide needed services to take on the added work emanating from the work created by the consortium.

Formal partnerships, on the other hand, result from mandates or the partners' desire to establish a framework that outlines goals, responsibilities, and financial arrangements. A review of five college partnerships formed as a result of government funding targeting the growth of research capacity in Ireland showed the creation of a centralized entity to oversee each partnership (Eddy, 2010a). Each alliance resulted in the creation of common policies regarding governance of the new venture and included clear objectives and goals. The reporting requirements of the government created an infrastructure that required annual evaluation of the partnerships, affording an opportunity for the group to assess its progress and make adjustments as needed. In this case, the overall outcome of the mandate to partner to receive funding resulted in increased research capacity in the country (Higher Education Authority, 2008).

In other cases, forced partnerships do not continue beyond the boundaries of the legislation or policies creating them. An alliance formed to create a network of two-year technical colleges fizzled when the initial funding stream dried up (Eddy, 2007). Although the prior competitive environment among the colleges shifted to become more collaborative based on the demands of the policy mandate, the motivation for continued cooperation vanished because supportive relationships were not built and college partners remained wary about the other partners.

The antecedents that preface the creation of a partnership matter. The history of the relationships of the partners casts a shadow on the current relationships, often making it easier for partners to work together because they are familiar with one another's work or because they have developed a shared understanding of the issue that they are working to address. In the case of informal partnerships, prior relationships are critical for the starting of the new ventures. Mandated partnerships, on the other hand, do not always benefit from familiarity that accompanies informal collaborations.

A critical starting element for partnerships is the amount of resources at their disposal. Resources can include expertise, facilities, technology capacity, or start-up funding. The ability to leverage these resources depends on the position of the partner in an organization and his or her own personal resources. Thornton and Shattuck (2006) reported how Housatonic Community College leveraged funds to foster an education and training alliance with the goal of addressing students' and businesses' workforce needs. Pooling resources is one benefit of partnering and works when all partners receive clear advantages. Another example showcasing the power of combining resources occurred in a strategic alliance among colleges, businesses, the state of Ohio, and the National Science Foundation. This consortium created a fuel cell prototyping center, with a primary outcome of creating economic development through building a specialization possible only through working with key partners (Diab, 2006). The amount of resources varies among partners, with more formal partnerships generally having more resources at their disposal.

Motivations

Another antecedent in the formation of partnership includes the motivating factors pushing partners to join together. Herzberg (1959) outlined a two-factor model of motivation. *Intrinsic motivation* emerges from a sense of self-driven reasons for engaging in an activity that may range from the need to fulfill personal needs to a desire to seek goals based on values such as honor, social status, idealism, or power. *Extrinsic motivation*, on the other hand, derives from external sources. These sources might come from money, coercion, mandates, or exertion of power. Collaborations involve a dance of numerous partners, some of whom are driven to participate given their internal desire to cooperate, whereas others become involved because they are told to by superiors or required by regulations. This mixture of motivations influences the course the partnership takes over time.

One extrinsic motivation for seeking out partners is to help cut institutional costs. Two means of saving resources are by jointly purchasing items and by sharing risks with the creation of insurance groups. According to Dorger (1999), barriers to success in sharing resources and costs include organizational inertia, unfamiliarity with the concept, differing resource and expectation levels, preferential treatment of one partner over another, and different organizational cultures and policies (pp. 73–74). On the other hand, support for these types of collaborative ventures comes from top administrators' buy in, trust built over time, focus on compromise, and creation of equity among partners (pp. 75–77). Another source of motivation involves seeking ways to save money by sharing expenses for technology (Sink, Jackson, Boham, and Shockley, 2004) or by using technology to create shared degree programs and delivery options (Godbey and Richter, 1999; Widmayer, 1999). Given the high costs of technology, collaboration in this arena is particularly helpful, as technology is constantly morphing and involves regular updating.

Conditions of economic exigency create a context ripe for collaborative efforts (Gray, 1989). Institutions are pressed to cut expenses and think more entrepreneurially about educational options. Watson and Jordan (1999) reported on a program developed by Texas Instruments that emerged to offer distance education and professional development. This program evolved into the creation of the Alliance for Higher Education, which helps member institutions reach more students through distance education. This partnership was initially driven by intrinsic motivations to advance corporate technology, but it became more extrinsically motivated when the company sought funded projects and partnerships using this technology.

Yet others (see, for example, Fahey, Ihle, Macary, and O'Callahan, 2007) develop partnerships to address students' success. Even though these motivations are often grounded in mandates such as No Child Left Behind or state higher education performance outcomes, it is the desire to support student learning that is at the core. Links with industry (Prigge, 2005) provide not only additional resources for colleges but also paths to the world of work for students. This combination of extrinsic and intrinsic motivations highlights the complex rationales for creating partnerships.

Some partnerships are formed to solve labor force shortages and leverage training. For instance, Golfin (1998) reported on the need for the Navy to have a pool of trained personnel. Workforce training programs like Tech Prep can provide a conduit for students to bridge the school-work divide as well as vocational training programs in community colleges. Business-school partnerships often exist on the fringes of institutions, with each partner having different needs and goals for the collaboration. Maintaining these tenuous relationships is complicated by the fact that educational improvement for the students is not always assessed (Hoff, 2002).

The Association of Governing Boards of Universities and Colleges advocates collaborations as a means to do more with less (Johnston and Noftsinger, 2004). The association's report underscores the rewards possible in consortia that seek mutual gains and notes the importance of trust and communications. At the same time, it is evident that struggles between partners will not go away. Yet the benefits from collaboration can help solve some of the complex challenges facing institutions and the grand challenges facing higher education. The motivations and rationales to partner contribute to long-term success.

Motivations also differ depending on the leader's level and position and the organization's size. Champions that provide the yeoman's work for starting a partnership are not always located at the top of the leadership chain (Watson, 2007) but often bring high intrinsic motivation to the venture.

Additionally, depending on institutional resources, some organizational partners may feel they have more at stake in joining a partnership (Eddy, 2007); thus, extrinsic rewards may motivate some partners more than others. The unequal distribution of personal and organizational power, resources, and sources of motivation may create challenges as the partnership develops. Those perceiving less benefit from participation are less motivated to participate compared with those with more motivation for the partnership to succeed.

Context

The context in which joint ventures are created influences their formation and the goals and objectives of the group; it also provides the environment in which the partnership develops. The environmental context can range from one that is stable and predictable to one that is dynamic and shifting. Depending on the scenario, motivations to partner vary. Ultimately, the types of goals established also rely on the context. Colleges in more desperate situations will be willing to seek out riskier objectives than organizations in stable situations that can accommodate planning to meet strategic goals. Those partners perceiving they will gain more in partnering may be willing to put up with less than ideal circumstances in the collaboration, as they have more at stake in working with others.

Organizational change often serves as an impetus for the creation of partnerships. In Kotter and Cohen's eight-step change model (2002), a sense of urgency establishes the initial momentum for the change process. Urgency may arise from the outside environment—the need to address economic issues, mandates from the state or federal government, the requirements of funders or accreditation associations—or from within by the force of leadership or institutional needs (Astin and Astin, 2000). Typically during a crisis, power and decision making revert to those in top-level positions (Leslie and Fretwell, 1996), making central leadership a key component in partnership development. Lacey and Kingsley (1988) prepared a guide for building working partnerships based on data collected on twenty-one work-educational partnership programs. Their findings mirror the change model proposed by Kotter and Cohen (2002), namely, that key issues included brokering, forming two groups

EXHIBIT 1
Change Models for Forming Partnerships

Kotter & Cohen (2002)	Lacey & Kingsley (1988)	Eddy (2010b)
Create a sense of urgency	Brokering around a problem	Verbalizing motivation and context for partnering (problem, mutual vision, mandates)
Build a guiding coalition	Finding the right players	Aligning social capital of champion and leveraging organizational capital; range of informal to formal
Create a vision		Establishing partnership goals and team governance
Communicate the change vision		Framing the partnership to stakeholders
Empower broad-based action	Building commitment through ownership	Negotiating conflicts
Generate short-term wins		Framing outcomes
Don't let up	Planning a partnership	Evaluating the process
Make change stick	Preserving the partnership	Institutionalizing the partnership—moving beyond the champion toward partnership capital

of the right players, building commitment through ownership, planning the partnership, and preserving the partnership. Exhibit 1 outlines the change process as it pertains to partnerships, showcasing the steps outlined by Kotter and Cohen (2002) and presented by Lacey and Kingsley (1988). Alignment is evident in the need to set the stage for the change process and the involvement of key stakeholders. In the eight-stage model outlined by Kotter and Cohen (2002), the added steps of creating a vision and communicating the plan are included. The remaining stages of the change models are similar in building buy in to the process and keeping to the task of the change outlined. The final column of the exhibit presents the stages of partnership outlined in this volume. The first step includes partnership formation that is driven by the motivation of the partners and the context present at the inception. The partners bring to the collaboration different levels of social and organizational capital (see the following two sections of this chapter). Communication is critical throughout partnership formation, as is the ability to negotiate conflicts that may arise. Ultimately, the creation of partnership capital develops in the final stages of the partnership process.

The setting for organizational change implies that systems shift from the status quo. Fullan (2001) holds that leaders must have a moral purpose driving their push for change. This purpose may be intrinsically motivated and guided by a desire to make a positive difference, but equally often leaders may be extrinsically motivated to change operations to obtain more resources for their institution or themselves. Next, Fullan argues that leaders need to understand the change process, though he contends that linear models such as that outlined by Kotter and Cohen (2002) do not accurately represent a dynamic change process. Leaders must also focus on the relationships involved in making change happen and work to keep employees informed of new information. Last, Fullan states that leaders must ultimately help followers make sense of the changing landscape through coherent communication. Leaders thus have a challenging role during times of change, as they must not only tolerate a level of disequilibrium to foster in others a motivation to change (Lewin, 1943) but also make sense of the situation for others involved in the process (Weick, 1995).

The different modes of change range from first-order change that involves incremental and predictable evolution to second-order change that is frame breaking and radical (Van de Ven and Poole, 1995). In second-order change, chaos theory shows that change happens at the cusp of uncertainty, with leaders finding themes amid the complexity (Poole and Van de Ven, 2004). Thus, the current context of uncertainty, complex organizational interactions, and shifting economics provides an environment conducive for change. That said, those leading and advocating for change must feel comfortable operating on the edge of chaos and be willing to work with others in making sense of the new environment. In the postindustrial era, Rost (1991) argued, change processes differ from those required in the modern era, when hierarchical bureaucracy offered predictable outcomes. Instead, Rost noted that a postmodern world relies more on collaboration, seeking a common good, addressing global issues, focusing on diversity in organizations and through participation, and using critical discourse to bring about consensus in decision making. It is within this rich cornucopia that partnerships develop.

Conclusion

The formation stage of partnerships is much like sowing multiple seeds. Some seeds will take root and blossom only once, others will wither before producing any products, and still others will be perennials that continue to produce over time. The context in which the partnership develops is critical because it sets the stage for ongoing efforts. Key elements in the formation process are the motivations of the partners. Motivations for joining a partnership may differ from those necessary to maintain the partnership (Worrall, 2007). Some partners are motivated to participate based on a need to accomplish a task, concern about going awry of a mandate, fear of survival, or presence of a moral purpose and vision to accomplish an objective.

Partnerships range from informal ventures to more formal affairs with operating procedures and governance systems. The formation stage is critical because it sets the stage for the partners' ongoing relationships. For some short-term partnerships, the partnership dissolves once the initial goal is achieved. Those desiring a more long-term collaboration need to focus on relationship building and the development of trust among members. Leaders play a key role in supporting partnerships, but initial champions for the partnership may be located throughout the organization (Watson, 2007). The following section highlights the role of the champion's social capital in developing the partnership.

Social Capital of the Champion

Champions supply a critical role in partnership formation. For the purposes of this discussion, a champion is defined as an individual who advocates for the development of a partnership and who brings together others to engage in the project. For instance, Cele's research (2005) found that an individual academic played a significant role in steering transformation research activities during the evolution of a twenty-one-year-old research partnership between the University of Cape Town and a regional business. The faculty member served as the champion of the project over time, bringing together the rest of the collaborators and helping to orchestrate the operations. Champions are not necessarily located in leadership positions, as this example points out. Watson (2007) found that only the superintendent of the high school involved in a partnership among a high school, community college, and public university held a leadership position. The other two partners were in staff positions in outreach departments, but each was interested in seeing the collaborative process succeed.

The role of champions is to envision the benefits of the partnership for all partners and to trumpet them as they persuade others of the project's merits. According to Kelman (1961), three methods of social influence are possible: compliance, identification, and internalization. Compliance is transactional in nature and occurs when a person believes that by going along with the champion he or she will be viewed favorably. Identification, on the other hand, happens when others see the champion as a role model and seek to emulate his or her behavior and meet his or her expectation. And internalization occurs when the values the champion represents aligns with those he or she is trying to influence. Champions may use all forms of influence to advocate for the partnership, but the associated motivations to partner differ. Compliance is associated with mandated partnerships in which the partners are externally motivated to go along with the champion. Identification or internationalization sources of influence, on the other hand, are more often associated with intrinsic sources of motivation and value alignment regarding the goals of the partnership. For example, Cooper and Mitsunaga (2010) studied international collaborations and found that the faculty champions were able to convince partners and their institutions to provide support for the projects. In this case, faculty members were able to engender influence when partners saw the faculty members as role models or believed in the same value system regarding education in international settings. The connections that a champion has make a difference in how much leverage he or she may have in the overall process. Social capital represents the interconnections individuals have with one another and between social networks (Coleman, 1988).

The levels of social capital held by each partner provide a critical ingredient in forming and maintaining partnerships. Definitions of social capital vary. Putnam (2000) argues that an individual's social capital can be leveraged to provide good to the larger community. Through the use of personal networks, access to resources, and personal knowledge, individuals can pull together a social network to solve local problems. Bourdieu (1983), on the other hand, reviewed three forms of capital—economic capital, cultural capital, and social capital. For the latter, he saw tangible links of an individual network as able to leverage resources, with an emphasis on the acquisition of resources. Coleman (1988) instead argued for a fluidity of social capital, stating that "it is not lodged either in the actors themselves or in physical implements of production" (p. S98). Thus, relationships among individuals take on heightened importance.

Social capital comprises multiple elements and may be generated differently by individual champions. One form of social capital depends on trustworthiness and the social environment. Coleman (1988) explains that trust is involved in that the obligations of the social actors will be repaid and that the environment in place dictates the extent of the obligations. Thus, the more obligations a person has accrued, the more social capital he has. "The density of outstanding obligations means, in effect, that the overall usefulness of the tangible resources of that social structure is amplified by their availability to others when needed" (Coleman, 1988, p. S103). For instance, Temple (2006) found that projects seeking to improve effectiveness of higher education institutions in transitional states created social capital in the organizations; further, it was through internal project development rather than externally directed project goals that outcomes were obtained. The density of internal relationships helped to accomplish project goals.

Trust is another key component of social capital (Coleman, 1988). Dovey (2009) explored the role of trust in innovative collaborations. He determined that collaborative learning practices are the foundation of idea generation and that the environment for these practices relies on social capital resources—like trust.

Thus, a key point for leaders is to create nurturing environments in which trust can blossom.

Another form of social capital comes from information channels; "information is important in providing a basis for action" (Coleman, 1988, p. S104). Strong ties in networks are central to decision making and enhance the speed at which information travels. Morgan (2006) points out that information is a source of power; thus, it serves well as a lever of social capital. Information acts as a conduit to pass along stories or data and therefore allows social capital to accrue that can be used to further goals. Social actors may serve as an information hub for several other individuals, and these relationships may be maintained as long as all benefit. Because information is free, it is a public good, as is the generation of social capital. The fact that social capital is a public good means this arena is underinvested, and often the power of social capital is not acknowledged. But when social capital is applied by the champions of a project, benefits are generated.

Granovetter (1983) further explored the roles of social networks and determined that the density of the ties of individuals to one another affected the amount of influence they had at their disposal. Thus, close ties and relationships created more density, whereas loose ties and weaker relationships created less density. Weak ties, however, are not without utility, as these relationships put individuals in contact with larger circles of individuals that represent perspectives different from the relationships found in close ties. Weak ties allow for connections between typically unconnected areas of a network. Thus, individuals with the ability to bridge more relationships possess cognitive flexibility outside their own circle. Indeed, the American Association of State Colleges and Universities (2004) argues for the creation of boundary spanners between K–12 schools and institutions of higher education. These individuals would have ties to both levels of educational providers and have social capital that makes them at home in both worlds, which ultimately allows for more cognitive flexibility in seeing more options for problem solutions along the educational continuum.

A graphic example of the relationships inherent in social capital highlights the key roles of density, centrality, information, and trust (see Figure 1). In this example, the density of relationships with others is represented by the size of

FIGURE 1
Social Capital

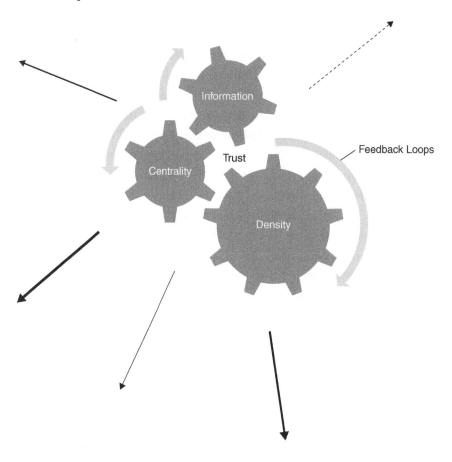

the shape, which in this case shows the shape that is largest in the set. The champion has greater social capital as a result of the number of obligations others owe to the person. Centrality represents how close the person is to key decision makers in the organization, whereas the final shape of information underscores the access the champion has to the flow of information within and outside the institution. The feedback loops in the diagram highlight the trust generated through relationships with the champion. The more trust available, the more social capital is able to grow and be put into motion. The connection the champion has with others is represented by the various arrows. Differences in the strength of relationships are highlighted by the thickness of the lines that connect the champion to others: stronger ties are represented by bolder lines, weaker ties by lighter or dashed lines.

Visualizing social capital provides a means of understanding the central components contributing to the creation of social capital. Some elements of social capital may be acquired once known. For instance, trust can be built among individuals based on interactions that show the ability to follow through on tasks, open communication, or create respect. Likewise, information sharing and listening skills represent components that help in the acquisition of social capital. Providing help for others begins to create a network of obligations. Sharing knowledge and expertise is just one example of how obligations can be created with others. Champions often have large amounts of social capital at their disposal that they can use to advance the creation of partnerships. Attention to building social capital can provide a lever for change and the needed resources necessary for creating a partnership.

Social network analysis provides a means to measure social capital among individuals (Figure 2). In this case, the nodes are the individuals and the connections between represent the ties—weak or strong. The more central an individual is to connections, the more ties to his or her node. In Figure 2, those central individuals are located in the densest parts of the figure. The largest node provides a critical role as a bridge to other areas of the social network, underscoring Granovetter's point (1983) of the strength of weak ties. It is just this type of bridging that allows for innovation. These central nodes represent the role of the champion in a partnership. Dallmer (2004) presented a personal account of her role in partnerships when working on improving teacher education practices in the field. She worked with two different universities and recounted how consensus building with a collaborative model was more effective than a top-down approach that imposes roles and goals for the collaboration. Here, the champion can leverage his or her social capital to get others to collaborate rather than having collaboration dictated by mandates. In the latter case, a single leader can influence only so much by wielding authority (Kelman, 1961).

Walton and Guarisco (2007) analyzed how knowledge flowed in a transnational educational partnership using social network analysis to map

FIGURE 2
Sample of Social Network Analysis

the relationships over time. The ten-year longitudinal study provided data on the establishment and evolution of the partnerships. The research found that feedback was central to sustaining the partnership, including feed-forward and feed-across knowledge transfer. In this case, the flow of information helped create shared learning in the network zone, ultimately providing for a means to institutionalize the knowledge gained over time. Use of the social networking analysis allowed for visual representation of the partnership's structures. Fang and Hung (2008), on the other hand, found in their research that only certain aspects of social capital combined with certain organizational learning to provide a context in which technology knowledge was transferred. In this case, the core network, high relation intensity, and shared values were critical components.

Generally, the champion has a great amount of social capital to facilitate the sharing of information among partners. In this position, the champion helps provide shape to the collaboration and the meaning attached to the goals and vision (Fairhurst and Sarr, 1996). Thus, who the champion is matters to the partnership. The same project may not gain a foothold without the right person with connections, access to resources, and credibility among partners. Vaughn (2009) reported on the role of the champion in the formation of a partnership and noted how the champion was able to leverage resources to form several nested partnerships in his organization. The institution thus served as the hub for a larger network, moving the concept of social network analysis up to a level where the institution rather than an individual served in the key node position to link other organizations together. These outcomes occurred only because of the social capital the champion possessed. A person with fewer connections or influence would not have obtained the same outcomes.

One way of considering the different roles in partnerships is to think of the partners as insider or outsider participants. Coburn, Bae, and Turner (2008) investigated insiders and outsiders and noted that authority and status affected the negotiations among participants in their research, with those in authority possessing a greater range of tools for negotiations. Indeed, they also pointed out, the links to access to organizational resources as the organizational structure of the district under study influenced outcomes. A champion who is central to decision making controls decisions on how to use resources. In this case, status as defined using titles has less to do with access to resources. A source of social capital for the champion is the ability to influence decision making regarding the use of resources.

Like other forms of capital, social capital is a resource that can diminish when it is spent, much like an IOU note. Once obligations between individuals have been satisfied, the amount of capital decreases. Thus, timing is important in the ways that capital is implemented. Eddy (2007) reported on a partnership among five colleges and noted that fear drove the establishment of the alliance. In the initial formation of the partnerships, the five college leaders worked together to press for the collaboration and were rewarded by increased state funding. Once the funding was spent, the motivation to continue the alliance diminished. Although three of the colleges would have liked to continue the alliance, their champions held less social capital than the other two college leaders who were pushing to dissolve the collaboration. The use of the partners' social capital early on in the partnership resulted in less capital available as time went on to sustain the relationships. Champions need to continue to replenish their social capital to maintain their influence and to help support the partnership over time.

Partners can leverage the use of social capital, given the important role it plays in partnership formation. First, champions can strategize how to expend the capital at their disposal as partnerships form, knowing that timing can make a difference in the venture's long-term success. Second, those in authority can work to create environments in which a culture of trust is built. More innovation can occur when individuals feel they are in a supportive environment. Even though fear can motivate some partners to participate in a collaboration, once the imminent threat in the environment is gone, nothing remains to hold the partnership together. Finally, information serves as a factor in the creation of social capital. How meaning is shaped can influence outcomes (Neumann, 1995). Thus, partners should invest time in creating shared meaning for the partnership and work to build common goals.

Organizational Capital

Social capital focuses on the resources at the disposal of individuals, whereas organizational capital focuses on the resources individuals can access that are generated in their institutions. Typically, organizational capital is thought of as a tangible resource. In this case, the capital might be space, technology, funding for materials, access to knowledge, or human resources. Access to organizational capital depends on the champion's centrality in an organization (Granovetter, 1983) and the density of relationships to leverage access to resources (Coleman, 1988). This section reviews fundamentals of organizations as they contribute to partnership development, including a review of organizational frames, power, and resources.

Organizational Frames

Organizations operate in different frames that hold some elements of operation more central than others. Bolman and Deal (2008) outlined four frames of organizations: structural, human resources, political, and symbolic. Each frame is built on a core set of beliefs that guide the organization and a set of practices that are central to operations. Particular types and forms of leadership exhibit more success in the frames as well. The fit between leaders and organizations is critical to success. Thus, understanding the ways in which the frames operate can provide insight into the best ways to partner in an institution.

In the structural frame, bureaucracy is at the core of operations. Weber (2009) was the first theorist to outline the elements in bureaucracies. He cited several key factors required for this type of organizational frame: a fixed division of labor, a hierarchy of offices, a set of rules for performance, a separation of personal from official property and rights, and technical qualifications to distinguish jobs. Modern industry was built on these ideals, with early factories and businesses showcasing strict organizational charts of leadership and repetition of job functions on factory lines. The goal of this frame was to run an efficient and productive organization that produced targeted outcomes. Work quotas were often developed to predict the levels of product to expect. Leaders in this frame focus on the allocation and coordination of work. Those leading in a structural frame rely on the organizational hierarchy to provide structure and a line of command, using rules and regulations to help guide behavior. Influence is primarily obtained by compliance (Kelman, 1961).

The human resource frame, on the other hand, holds the role of people in the organization as a central focus. Instead of an emphasis on the structure of operations, it is the relationship of the people to the organization that is most important. The Hawthorne studies (Gillespie, 1993) were conducted to determine the impact of the structural element of lighting in the environment on production levels, but they ultimately revealed that it was the attention to the human element of the production process, namely the factory worker, that resulted in more output. This research ushered in a focus on the human element of the organization. An underlying assumption here is that organizations exist to serve human needs rather than the reverse (Bolman and Deal, 2008). Instead of seeing people as mere cogs in the machinery of an organization, researchers acknowledged the symbiotic relationship between people and organizations—they need each other. Human resources are viewed as central to organizational operations. In this frame, leaders believe in and trust people, are accessible and visible, and empower others (Rost, 1991). The type of influence evident is identification and internalization (Kelman, 1961).

The political frame focuses on the level of conflict inherent in institutions that serve individuals with multiple interests. "Conflict arises whenever interests collide" (Morgan, 2006, p. 167). Leaders in this case need to focus on how to deal with this conflict by providing space and processes that allow conflicting perspectives to be resolved. In a politically oriented organization, divergent interests play out, with individuals forming dominant coalitions around interests that coalesce regarding a particular issue or project outcome (Morgan, 2006). These coalitions are fluid, with the driving factor for bringing actors together changing over time. For example, a partnership may form in a political frame as the result of a match in ideologies or a desire to seek similar outcomes of a particular policy (Fowler, 2009). State mandates for K–16 partnerships provide one forum in which these types of partnerships might develop.

A critical element in the political frame is the role of power. Power is used to seek influence in the organizational system and to leverage a particular position in a conflicting situation. "A strong case can also be made for the idea that, although everyone has access to sources of power, ultimate power rests with the people or forces that are able to define the stage of action on which the game of politics is played" (Morgan, 2006, p. 213). As outlined in the preceding section on social capital, individuals can wield their own power to garner particular outcomes. Likewise, in an organization, those who can effectively negotiate in the contested environment can leverage outcomes that best meet their needs. Adaptive leaders (Heiftez, 1994) can use their influence in a variety of manners in a political frame. Skills in negotiating conflict and possession of enough power and influence to dictate actions contribute to leading in this framework. Knowing the environment and being able to be flexible based on the situation links well with leading using contingency theory (Fiedler, 1967). In this case, the type of leadership needed for a given scenario shifts. Being politically savvy allows for an awareness of what type of leadership is required at the time.

The final frame relies on understanding the culture of an organization and leveraging the use of symbolism in operations. One can imagine the organization like a theater in which actions are on display and carried out. Leaders can create the theaters in use or make use of those already in place. Tierney (1991) reviewed the role of organizational culture for higher education. He focused on how leaders can make use of time, space, and communication to help shape the culture. According to Clark (1972), the creation of an organizational saga begins to reinforce the culture of an institution. How leaders tell the institution's story draws attention to different aspects of operations (Eddy, 2003; Neumann, 1995). The same holds true for a partnership. How the story regarding the urgency that creates the partnership (Kotter, 2008) is relayed and how the idea of the collaboration is portrayed shape the development and sustainability of the partnership. Often in recounting stories of the creation of a partnership, participants recollect key moments that were pivotal for the group (Reed, Cooper, and Young, 2007). How leaders tell the partnership story and what aspects they reinforce shift the focus of support for the collaboration. The saga may be such that individuals feel aligned with the partnership's goals, allowing the leader to internalize a shared value system with others (Kelman, 1961).

Leadership exists along a continuum ranging from authoritative to collaborative in nature. Goleman (2000) outlined six different styles of leadership emanating from the elements contained in his theory of emotional intelligence: coercive, authoritative, affiliative, democratic, pacesetting, and coaching. The approaches that demand particular behaviors from others (coercive and pacesetting) generally have a negative impact on the organizational culture. When people are placed in the center of operations and decision making, more positive impacts on culture and operations occur. Similar to this array of leadership behaviors, Amey and Brown (2004) developed an interdisciplinary collaboration model based on various stages of development. Their model starts with leadership behaviors being directive and moves to a style in which leaders act more as facilitators. From here, leadership behavior further evolves to be inclusive and ultimately results in being servant oriented. The interdisciplinary collaboration model further highlights the shift from an individual orientation to a group process to a collaborative orientation (Amey and Brown, 2004). Like in the interdisciplinary model developed by Amey and Brown to show collaborative efforts in an organization, a shift in

EXHIBIT 2
Organizational Frameworks and Leadership Behaviors

Frames (Bolman and Deal, 2008)	Leadership Styles (Goleman, 2000)	Interdisciplinary Leadership (Amey and Brown, 2004)
Structural: Hierarchy, organizational structure, rules and policies	Authoritative	Directive
Human Resources: People centered, relationships, nurturing, cobeneficial	Affiliative Democratic	Facilitative
Political: Conflict, competing interests, dominant coalitions, power	Coercive Pacesetting	Inclusive
Symbolic: Theater, symbols, organizational saga, stories	Coaching	Servant oriented

orientation occurs over time in partnerships developed between institutions. As collaborations develop between and among institutions, a move to a new configuration results; in this new entity, partnership capital may emerge. This type of capital is distinct from social or organizational capital and is addressed more fully in the next section.

Even though the organizational frames outlined above may include a range of leadership behaviors, the organizational structure of the frames emphasizes some styles of leadership over others. Exhibit 2 presents a summary of the frames and suggests the types of leadership behavior typical in each.

Just as particular types of leadership may be more aligned in the organizational frames, so too are different forms of power. Partners are able to tap into organizational capital, depending on the organizational frame in operation, the type of leadership in place, and the levels of power available. Thus, although individuals can bring certain forms of social capital to a partnership, the amount of organizational capital available to a partnership depends on the routes of access to the resources available, the size of the institution, and the leadership of the organization. The following section reviews the range of power levers available for use in organizational capital.

Power

Various forms of power may be used as a resource or to provide access to other resources. Power occurs at an individual level, as noted in the section on social capital, but is also available in an institution. Etzioni (1964) outlined a series of organizational types and associated powers: coercive, calculative, and normative. Expanding on this topology, French and Raven (1960) outlined five sources of power: referent (charismatic), expert, legitimate, reward, and coercive. Charismatic power is generated from within an individual and draws others to action in a desire to please the referent leader or because of a desire to be like the person (Weber, 2009). Expert power, on the other hand, results from having knowledge or information that others need to accomplish a task. For a partnership, a faculty member may have expert power because of his or her knowledge of a particular area or skill in application of different kinds of technology. For instance, in the partnership outlined by Cooper and Mitsunaga (2010), the faculty members involved possessed power because of their knowledge of language, culture, and disciplinary bases.

Legitimate power is acquired as the result of position or role (Weber, 2009). Thus, college and community leaders have access to organizational capital merely because of their positions of authority. This power may be used to encourage or influence others to join a partnership or may be used to give legitimacy to efforts begun by a faculty champion. The partnership outlined by Watson (2007) showed that even though the community college champion was a staff member, the partnership was sanctioned by the college president and given more credence when this level of approval and acknowledgment was obtained. Reward power is at the heart of transactional leadership—if one acts in a particular manner, he will be rewarded for that behavior. Rewards may take a variety of forms, from recognition of efforts to extra salary to activities that support tenure and promotion. Generally, compliance occurs when rewards are present but disappears when the rewards are no longer given (Kelman, 1961). Finally, leaders use coercive power to force someone to do something they do not want to do. Negative connotations are associated with using coercive power to obtain actions; this type of power if associated with dictators who use it for intimidation.

Organizational actors have a range of power sources at their disposal to influence those in the organization as well as to make resources available to collaborative efforts. As outlined by French and Raven (1960), some power sources are the result of position and authority in the institution. The review of partnerships throughout this volume, however, highlights a number of partnerships that flourish without top-level involvement, in particular at the inception of the partnership. Looking at a wider range of power sources provides a means to understand partnership development more fully.

Morgan (2006) identified fourteen forms of power in organizations. Like other typologies of power, some of the power is the result of position in an organization, but other sources of power are available regardless of position. Each aspect of power can be accessed in different manners in the four organizational frames outlined earlier, with some of the power emanating from the features being greater in particular frames. Each facet of Morgan's power levers is discussed in the following paragraph, with attention paid to how they might manifest in the different organizational frameworks and who might have access to each particular power.

Formal authority. Power from formal authority emerges from Weber's idea of legitimate power in an organization (2009). In modern organizations, formal authority is ordained by position and the attendant responsibilities that go with it. Thus, those higher in the hierarchy have more formal authority and thus more power. The structural frame in particular draws power based on formal authority, as the core organizational philosophy is based on the organizational hierarchy and structure. Formal authority is also available to those leading volunteer organizations or community groups, as these individuals also are recognized leaders even if they are not in paid positions. As such, volunteers can be leaders in partnerships using the power they have access to from their position in the group.

Control of scarce resources. As noted earlier, the motivation to save resources is a driving force in the creation of some partnerships. Therefore, those who can control the acquisition of the resources have power in the collaboration. In formal organizations, those in certain positions are able to determine how resources are used. Typically, these positions are located at the top of the organization, but employees are well aware of the power in the possession of the administrative assistants who control supplies. Each organizational frame uses control of resources: the structural frame administers resources using rules, the human resource frame views people as the greatest resource, the political frame allocates resources based on political clout, and the symbolic frame views resources as the control of meaning and symbols. In volunteer organizations, prime resources are the volunteers and the expertise and labor they can supply. Partners bring different levels of resources to the partnership, and those with more access to the resources have more power.

Use of organizational structure, rules, and regulations. The use of organizational structure and rules is most aligned with the structural frame. Partners operating in institutions using this structure garner power by knowing how to use the rules to their advantage. Power might come from knowing the process of policies; for instance, knowing the details of the curricular process can provide an advantage in creating a joint degree program. Likewise, the political frame uses the policy process as a means to garner power. In this case, the formation of the regulations can provide preference for particular actors in the organization. Forming coalitions to help sway the policy formation in a particular manner is a key element in the political frame.

Control of decision making. Having influence over the decision-making process can provide the leverage needed when institutional support is sought for a partnership. In a structural frame, decision making is controlled in the hierarchy, with those farther up on the organizational chart having more control over decision making. Institutions supporting a human resource frame value and nurture people; thus, they make decisions that support this goal. Often in this frame, more collegial forms of decision making are evidenced. Control over decisions in the political frame, however, is most influenced by the formation of dominant coalitions. The fluid nature of the negotiation process might mean that particular factions are pulled together, depending on the issues; thus, the outcomes are more unpredictable. Influence over decision making in the symbolic frame, on the other hand, focuses more on perceptions. Thus, leaders adept at providing meaning and helping to make sense of an issue have the greatest influence over decision making, often regardless of position.

Control of knowledge and information. As outlined in the section on social capital, knowledge is power. Control of information provides a lever of influence because knowing particular information in advance or understanding the impact of knowledge on processes before others provides an advantage of time to make institutional adjustment. Individuals throughout the institution can accrue knowledge and information. Even though institutions operating in a structural frame might control the flow of information based on the level of position in the organization, the informal network in operation begins to level the field in this frame. The coin of the realm in the political frame is information and knowledge. Members of different coalitions have different types of knowledge, which results in particular coalition formations, depending on issues. How the information is framed concerns those operating in a symbolic frame. It is the spin in this case versus the information itself that is central.

Control of boundaries. The ability to control the playing field helps limit the players who can participate in decision making and ultimately in reaping rewards. Rules govern the structural frame and are used to control boundaries. Likewise, it is through the use of coalitions that the boundaries are guarded in a political organization. In this case, however, the borders are fluid and change over time, depending on the context. Those once on the outside of the process may find themselves at the center as the context shifts and the other attributes they bring to the table are now valued.

Ability to cope with uncertainty. Both the political frame and the symbolic frame are set up to handle uncertainty better. In the political frame, the shifting nature of coalitions and the different forms of conflict require adaptability. Flexibility in compromising when working with others to obtain an overarching objective creates an environment in which uncertainty is tolerated. In the symbolic frame, any uncertainty may be given new meaning, depending on how it is framed. As Neumann (1995) exemplified in her research on two colleges, how the campus perceives uncertainty is influenced by how the leader frames the change. In her research, one campus president led a campus with more resources at its disposal, but campus members perceived the overall environment to be dire. On the other hand, the other campus president framed the situation on campus as one full of possibilities, when in fact the campus was under more resource constraints. For the latter president, dealing with uncertainty and framing the situation positively for campus members resulted in a more optimistic view of the future.

Control of technology. The use of technology is one motivation for partnering; thus, control of this resource provides power. Technology covers a broad continuum, from simple applications of a slide projector to high-level computing that requires a national grid system to create a platform able to support sophisticated data manipulations. In the sciences, technology to outfit labs is costly and often requires particular space constraints. Because of the continuum, various levels of power are generated based on the level of technology controlled and that desired by others. In a structural frame, a particular department or faction of the organization would control technical information. In a human resources frame, technology would be controlled by those most skilled in the area, whereas in the political frame, technology control would be a negotiated item and the coalition controlling technology would be most powerful when this resource is needed and less powerful when it was not.

Interpersonal alliances, networks, and control of informal organizations. Social networks exist in organizations just as they do among organizations. Individuals tied into internal networks gather more capital. These alliances are not necessarily tied to position but are based on connections, information sharing, and reliance to fulfill job functions. Thus, two individuals in the same position may have different levels of power based on how they have developed their networks. Informal organizations exist in all frameworks but may be most valued in human resource and political frames because they reward interpersonal relationships.

Control of counterorganizations. Leaders in a structural frame would use rules and policies to control counterorganziations, but these informal networks would still give power to those leading at this informal level. Political players would welcome counterorganizations into the fold when it is worthwhile for the overall goal. Because the formation of coalitions is fluid, those currently considered a counterorganization may one day become a welcome partner. The context affects the perception of this element.

Symbolism and the management of meaning. Clearly, the symbolic frame garners the most power by managing meaning. Berger and Luckmann (1966) posited that the interactions that occur on an individual level shape meaning in organizations. Weick (1995) created a model of sense making that underscored how the meaning of reality might be shaped by leaders to help give meaning for others. Reality might be influenced by the telling of stories, the creation of logos and slogans, and the creation of a common vision to which the organization aspires. Partners who are able to create a plausible vision for others may ultimately have more influence than those in control of tangible resources.

Gender and the management of gender relations. Gender is often a basis of power, typically with men having more power by default (Morgan, 2006). Acker (1990) coined the concept of gendered organizations to define how male norms dictate the distribution of power. Organizations are the "products and producers of gender-based power relations, and . . . masculine ways of doing things are inherent in structural, ideological and symbolic aspects of organization, as well as in everyday interactions and practices" (Hatch and Cunliffe, 2006, p. 274). When organizational structures favor men, power accrues in a particular way. Therefore, the gender of the partners can mean access to more or less power in the institution. The power of gender crosses all organizational frames, but the structural frame reinforces more of the hierarchical norms that reward men.

Structural factors that define the stage of action. Underlying structural patterns governing culture define the stage for actions. Thus, societal influences of economics, class, and race have large impacts on organizations.

Understanding how these factors affect the stage of action can give partners insight into the limits of the other sources of power at their disposal.

The power one already has. Power begets power. Those possessing power are able to acquire more power because they have multiple levers of access at their disposal. The previous illustrations of power sources highlight how those in positions of authority or who control information and meaning making garner power. Inherent in this organizational form of power are elements of individual social capital. Individuals throughout the organization have varying degrees of social capital and have power in their own right outside that bestowed in their institutional context. Individuals located in all frames have varying degrees of this form of power. Exhibit 3 summarizes the various forms of power and highlights how each is manifested in the four organizational frames. Consequently, even though many power sources are evident in multiple frames, they operate in different manners in the frames. In partnership formation, the type of power available for use to the partnership varies depending on what the partners involved might access. Differences in organizational capital are apparent based on the differences in accessible power of the key partners. For instance, if one partner operates in a structural frame and is in a high-level position, the type of power he can access is greater than that of another partner located in a similar type of organization but in a position markedly lower in the organizational hierarchy. Likewise, a partner located in a symbolic organization may have power and influence based on how she can shape meaning for others but may not have direct control over resources. Importantly, followers' expectations and behaviors influence the partners' power (Morgan, 2006). The next section reviews the various forms of resources that partners can access in organizations.

Resources

The resources available in organizations provide an integral form of capital that can help support partnerships. One of the motivations to partner is to pool resources and use them efficiently. Tangible resources include access to funding, space, and people. Partners have different access to these types of resources, often based on the type of organizational frame in operation and

EXHIBIT 3
Morgan's Sources of Power

Type of Power	Use Within Frames
Formal authority	Structural: Positions
Control of scarce resources	Structural: Rules
	Human Resources: People
	Political: Political clout
	Symbolic: Meaning and symbols
Use of organizational structure, rules, and regulations	Structural: Bureaucracies
	Political: Policy influence
Control of decision processes	Structural: Hierarchy
	Human Resources: Collegial
	Political: Dominant coalitions
	Symbolic: Perceptions of reality
Control of knowledge and information	Structural: Position/authority
	Political: Negotiating chip
	Symbolic: Framing/spin
Control of boundaries	Structural: Rules
	Political: Changing coalitions
Ability to cope with uncertainty	Political: Alliance swings
	Symbolic: Social construction of reality
Control of technology	Structural: Division responsibility
	Human Resources: Expertise
	Political: Coalition oversight
Interpersonal alliances, networks, and control of informal organization	Human Resources: Relationships
	Political: Networks
Control of counterorganizations	Structural: Rules and policies
	Political: Collaboration as needed
Symbolism and the management of meaning	Symbolic: Sense making and framing
Gender and the management of gender relations	All frames: Typically reward male norms
Structural factors that define the stage of action	All frames: Cultural influences of race, class, gender
The power one already has	All frames: Individual social capital

Source: Morgan, 2006.

the levels of power at the disposal of each partner. The difference in access to organizational capital between partners sets the stage for inequities.

In his evaluation of a university service-learning partnership with a nonprofit organization, Bushouse (2005) found that the resource constraints at the nonprofit meant that university students' participation cost less than the staff time committed to oversight. The high rates of returns provided a clear benefit to the nonprofit but presented differences in the amount of power in the possession of the nonprofit relative to the university. Thus, universities must address these differences before entering these types of partnerships. Preexisting organizational characteristics can affect the partnership (Edens and Gilsinan, 2005). In the case of resource differentials, a threat of inequity evolves in which the resource-rich partners have power over the partner with fewer resources. Some of this gap in resources may be bridged if the champion for the project has enough social capital to lessen the impact.

Resources can provide leverage in the partnership, but they can also show the differentials between partners that may lead to problems in the relationship's stability. As the partnership develops, it is important to discuss the levels of commitment of resources each partner brings to the collaboration. The pooling of resources can help in creating capacity and thereby the ability to accomplish more by partnering.

Conclusion

Partners have access to different forms of organizational capital. The type of organizational framework in place provides different levers that can be used in developing and sustaining partnerships. Each organizational frame in operation emphasizes different factors: for the structural frame, rules and structure are central; for the human resources frame, people are central; for the political frame, negotiating conflicts among different coalitions is central; and for the symbolic frame, using symbols to frame meaning for others is central. Inequities often occur among partners, given power differentials. Several sources of power are available for individuals to use to access resources and to support the formation and development of partnerships. Differences in power and resources lead to inequities between partners that must be resolved to sustain a partnership. How individuals use power provides access to resources and organizational capital for the partnership. Those with less organizational capital at their disposal have less power to negotiate for their desires, but how the power in possession is used can still move the partnership forward. Miller (2005) reviewed a university-community-school partnership using the lenses of power and privilege to evaluate the collaborative efforts. He used Freire's dialogical framework for analysis to determine whether the partnerships were authentically mutual or horizontal or, instead, were inequitable in power relations and thus partners' roles. In the final analysis, Miller found community groups often were at a disadvantage.

As partnerships develop, social capital and organizational capital combine to facilitate joint operations. Champions can access their personal networks to help start a partnership and tap into the organizational capital at their disposal once a partnership is started. Knowing the types of capital available can give those seeking to develop a partnership a variety of levers to help in forming collaborations.

Partnership Capital

Partnership capital forms after a collaborative effort moves beyond a mere collection of individual partners' interests to a sense of shared norms that guide the venture. Partnership capital is created from the synergy of the individual partners. In Figure 3, two partners are represented in the Venn diagram. The darker shaded area where the circles overlap illustrates the nexus of partnership capital. Here, the development of mutual interests, common goals, and shared meaning of language occurs. Open communication allows an opportunity to process conflicts and negotiate the ultimate goals. This process is ongoing and dynamic. It is important to attend to these details to sustain the partnerships. Often at this stage, elements of the partnership become institutionalized.

It is in the intersecting overlay of the individual partners that partnership capital forms. When individual partners move past individual interests to common goals and mission, partnership capital forms. It is the strength of social networks that fosters the development of social capital among partners in these collaborations. Through the formation of partnership capital, a capacity is

FIGURE 3
Partnership Capital

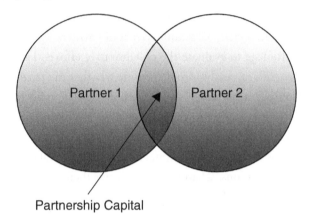

Partnership Capital

created that could not be obtained alone or by the mere sharing of resources. Over time, shared norms are created among partners that form as a result of negotiation, time together to build trust, and shared knowledge and meaning for ideas and visions regarding the joint venture. In the process of institutionalizing the partnership, it moves beyond the individual partners and organizations and becomes a different construct, namely partnership capital.

Supporting Elements
Several key elements help to support successful collaborations. Baus and Ramsbottom (1999) reported on several factors: "shared vision, clearly defined goals, a focus on real problems, an institutionalized decision-making structure, local decision making, continuity among partnership personnel, systematic communication with all partners and with the community, sufficient time for institutional change to occur, the provision of resources to those whose roles and relationships will change, and the provision of professional development training" (pp. 4–5). Leaders can help guide partnerships to obtain the important features that enable collaborations to succeed. Taking the time to develop shared goals for the group is important. Setting up routes of communication and feedback loops helps assure that all partners have shared meaning about what the partnership symbolizes. Another aspect of a partnership is the creation of

a neutral third party that is apart from either institution (Baus and Ramsbottom, 1999). This neutral space allows for the creation of partnership capital, because the partners work together to create something new. This capacity provides what Heifetz (1994) terms "adaptive space." In this adaptive space, a context is provided in which negotiations can occur and a sense of trust can grow. Clearly, the perspectives each partner brings to the partnership influence how this space is used.

A convergence of efforts can occur through coordination of state and federal policymakers. The creation of P–16 collaborations provides an example of how partnerships can be affected through the coordination of policy efforts. Here, partnership capital can grow from the joint venture, but challenging old boundaries to form new partnerships is required (American Association of Colleges for Teacher Education, 2005). The breakdown of old patterns of individual behavior requires the creation of trust. If the partners come into the venture looking only at short-term goals, it is unlikely that trust will have the time or space to develop in the group. The development of joint knowledge, however, helps build capacity in partnerships (Zeelen and van der Linden, 2009).

Shinners (2006) examined a university and public school partnership and determined that over time leadership emerged among partners that focused on supporting the partnership's goals rather than the individual goals of either institutional collaborator. The shift to the goals of the partnership over the institution was pivotal. Although another key to long-lasting success is leadership's involvement at critical stages, partners have different levels of involvement and accompanying influence in the process. The maturation of a partnership allows for the building of trust and the testing of relationships. According to Shinners (2006), skills and strategies were developed over time to support partnership goals in the adaptive space created.

Challenges to Partnerships

Several challenges exist to the sustainability of partnerships and the creation of partnership capital. All stages of burgeoning partnerships have conflicts and tensions. The initial euphoria of the conception of partnering gives way to the realities of working with multiple individuals, conflicting ideals, and differing

FIGURE 4
Push-and-Pull Factors of Partnerships

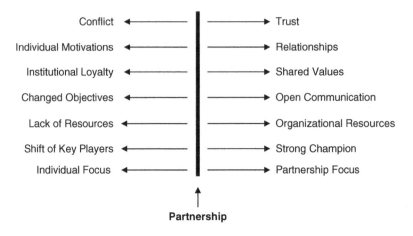

expectations and resources. Like Lewin's force field analysis for change (1943) that highlights forces working against one another, a similar tug-of-war occurs throughout the formation and development of partnerships (see Figure 4). Challenges occur when partnerships are created from grant funding; the resource stream may be limited and create tensions if the partnership is not self-sustaining and additional funding is not forthcoming. The turnover of personnel in a partnership may disrupt the partnership. In particular, when the champion is no longer present, a key advocate for the partnership is missing, which may jeopardize the collaboration.

The creation of a partnership creates a separate space for individual partners to operate. A drawback of this "other" status of the partnership is that the parties involved may have less investment in the collaboration, focusing instead on individual institutional needs. The pull of institutional loyalties often outweighs the benefits acquired by collaborating. Without the common goals or visions pushing the partners to collaborate, the pull away from the partnerships becomes too great and the venture fails.

Actions involved in educational reform partnerships often assume a shared understanding of terms used, but as Fraser (2006) found, individuals often have different conceptions of meaning for terms that may undermine obtaining goals. Thus, a challenge emerges in creating a shared understanding of the reasons for partnering and ways of talking about the collaboration. Without this shared understanding, the tensions pressing against the partnership become too great and the partnership collapses.

Conclusion

Not all partnerships result in the creation of partnership capital. As evidenced by the number of partnerships that fail (Farrell and Seifert, 2007; Reed, Cooper, and Young, 2007), the creation of partnership capital occurs on more rare occasions. Sustaining and institutionalizing partnerships leads to the creation of partnership capital and the capacity to move beyond the range of possibilities for individual partners operating alone. Various factors can support the creation of partnership capital, including the creation of a shared vision and goal, open communications, and the presence of trust. Without these critical elements, partnerships are challenged. When individual interests override those present in the partnership, the joint collaboration fails. Individual partners can concentrate on the support elements to help sustain partnerships and create partnership capital. Partnership capital is created only as a result of multiple partners' involvement but is not possessed by any one partner. The shared network, values, and vision in partnership capital provide the fundamental elements to help sustain partnerships and are key to long-term sustainability.

Individual Collaborations

COLLABORATIONS ALSO OCCUR OUTSIDE the confines of institutional involvement, primarily in traditional forms of faculty work. It is often in this individual work, however, that collaborations have their roots. As a result of this genesis of partnerships from initial work by individual faculty, it is important to understand the roles of original collaborators and how these links may progress to form institutional partnerships. This section of the volume provides a review of the roles of collaborators to understand better the key elements for successful collaborations.

First, an overview highlights faculty collaborations. Specific references to other sources of research on this topic are included for those more interested in how these individual roles develop. Next, the role of faculty champions is reviewed to show how those without administrative line responsibilities serve in the development of larger partnerships. Faculty roles are important to consider, because how faculty think of the collaborations affects the final process. For instance, one view is to see the individual value of faculty work in a partnership rather than valuing the joint products of the process. The structures of the faculty reward system contribute to how some faculty members thus value their contributions. How faculty work is reviewed in the promotion and tenure process begins to set the stage for faculty collaborations.

The ways in which faculty operate are influenced by a number of factors, including disciplinary orientations, institutional type, and organizational culture. Some departments in the university value collaboration more than others. As an example, it is quite common in the sciences to have multiple researchers contributing to a research project and the resulting publications.

The humanities, on the other hand, more often value single-authored books that require faculty to work independently. The increased focus on interdisciplinary work, though, and the pressure to collaborate require faculty and institutions alike to reevaluate traditional norms and behaviors.

Partnerships, regardless of the level at which they are formed, may affect individual faculty work. The creation of joint degree programs affects the allocation of faculty resources between home college course coverage and courses offered in the collaboration. It is important to consider how this collaborative work is accounted for—through governance processes created for the partnership or by shifts in the home college's policies.

Faculty as Collaborators

Faculty members are the backbone of colleges and universities and provide students, parents, and other stakeholders with the face of the institution. The composition of faculty ranks is shifting, with more part-time adjunct faculty teaching students than in the past (Baldwin and Chronister, 2001). Thus, full-time faculty members must assume more of the responsibilities for academic leadership and governance. Additionally, role shifts for faculty are expanding, pressing faculty to bring in grant funding, publish more to help increase the prestige of the university, to use more interdisciplinary and collaborative learning techniques in teaching, and to contribute leadership in the academic ranks (Gappa, Austin, and Trice, 2007). Moreover, faculty work is also under increased scrutiny by administrators seeking to cut costs, because personnel costs account for 80 percent of university budgets (College Board, 2009).

Boyer (1990) argued for expanded conceptions of faculty research, positing four types of scholarship instead of a single means of evaluation. The traditional concept of research is represented in Boyer's typology in the scholarship of discovery, but expanded forms of scholarship include the scholarship of teaching, the scholarship of integration, and the scholarship of application. Despite the rhetoric of valuing expanded forms of faculty work, the currency of the reward structure still predominantly rewards traditional research (Fairweather, 2005). Thus, a bind exists for faculty members as collaborators. On the one hand, research is valued over teaching as evident in faculty salary distributions. On the other hand, collaborative efforts require an investment of time that may take away from research productivity. One means to bridge this divide is to collaborate on research projects. This approach, however, rewards certain disciplinary areas over others. The data-driven disciplines provide a more fertile ground for collaborations than literature or the humanities (Austin and Baldwin, 1991).

According to Austin and Baldwin (1991), faculty collaborations take root in both research and teaching. The authors point out that differences in status and power held by faculty collaborators influence joint ventures, much like institutional partnerships are affected. Junior faculty, women, and minorities typically have less power in collaborations with more senior colleagues, who are often white men. It becomes important then to negotiate the ground rules for the collaboration upfront. Austin and Baldwin suggested several steps: choosing colleagues or team members, dividing the labor, establishing work guidelines, and terminating the collaboration (p. 6). These stages mirror those suggested for institutional partnerships and serve to provide a template for faculty members participating in their own work before bridging to institutional partnerships.

Creamer (1999, 2004, 2005) has researched faculty collaborations from a number of perspectives, including collaboration with intimate partners, long-term collaborations, and evaluation of collaborations. The latter topic is of particular interest for partnership work, because how faculty members are rewarded for their collaborative efforts may serve as a source of motivation to partner. Creamer (2005) found that current promotion and tenure processes typically do not reward collaborative research; thus, collaborations often are not encouraged for junior faculty members or those seeking promotion. This institutional policy runs counter to institutional demands that expand faculty work (Gappa, Austin, and Trice, 2007) and serves to dissuade faculty from collaborating.

Nonetheless, faculty members continue to collaborate despite the lack of formal institutional rewards. Lattuca and Creamer (2005) argued that faculty collaborations should be analyzed from a learning perspective. This lens provides a different vantage point from that evaluating collaborative work from a cost-benefit perspective and can shed light on different sources of motivation for faculty working together. For example, in their review of a mandated collaboration to align leadership preparation programs in New Jersey, Goduto, Doolittle, and Leake (2008) found that the seventeen preparation programs established a chapter of the National Council of Professors of Educational Administration. This chapter created a learning community of field practitioners and allowed the group to challenge the values and beliefs about training, ultimately resulting in the revision of the preparation programs. When the focus is on the learning process rather than a measure of the value for promotion, positive outcomes are evident.

It is important to note that the majority of research on faculty productivity takes place in the context of research universities. Faculty members in other institutional types operate under different conditions and reward structures. For instance, community college faculty members have higher teaching responsibilities and little expectation for research (Townsend and Twombly, 2007). Given the context of the community college (Cohen and Brawer, 2008), however, faculty are expected to help support community development. This required outreach creates a ready environment for collaboration not always available in other institutional types.

Further research on faculty collaborations highlights the utility of reflective practice to investigate the learning process (Boud and Walker, 1993). Critically reflecting on learning means that assumptions are challenged and current beliefs tested (Brookfield, 1995; Tennant and Pogson, 1995). Joint reflective practices involve metacognitive practices. "Metacognition refers to higher order thinking, which involves active control over the cognitive processes engaged in learning" (Livingston, 1997, para. 1). In this case, faculty members reflect on their own learning as a result of the collaboration but also question how the learning can result in changes and adaptations to the collaborative process. Ultimately, metacognitive practices can help develop thought communities (Damrosch, 2000; John-Steiner, 2000) comprising scholars who have worked together over long periods of time. These thought communities may serve as the roots for institutional collaborations as well, as they represent a cadre of members who have strong relationships and connections.

Traditional research on faculty collaborations focused on particular functions of the group. Because faculty members are rewarded for their productivity, author order and credit (Austin and Baldwin, 1991; Speigel and Keith-Spiegel, 1970) take on heightened importance. Embedded in this ordering of authors are ethical considerations and power dynamics that influence the order, often with senior faculty holding prominence over junior faculty or graduate students (Bridgwater, Bornstein and Walkenbach, 1981; McGinn and others, 2005). Recent research on a faculty collaboration (Hinck and others, 2009) found that the creation of group space was critical to the process. Several components contributed to the formation of this group space, including building the relationship (Adler and Kwon, 2002), building trust (Bryk and Schneider, 2002), and crossing boundaries (Holley, 2009).

As with other group development processes (Tuckman, 1965), tensions are evident in the formation of faculty collaborations. Hinck and others (2009) identified a number of tensions affecting the creation of their group space. Tensions included the recognition of an initial hierarchy based on faculty position (Morgan, 2006). With position came initial levels of power in the group. Additional pressures affecting the group were time constraints (Sorcinelli, 2000), as group members had to choose to elevate the work of the group over competing demands on their time. The research of Hinck and others ultimately found that the use of group space allowed for redefining intellectual community. Key to this shift was valuing the process of group work and the thought community (John-Steiner, 2000) over product generation (Creamer, 2004). The time spent together as a group resulted in changes in conception of the group's goals and the bonds holding the team together (Wood, 1996). Of note, this type of adaptive space creation mirrors that involved for creating partnership capital.

Faculty members also work in collaborations with others outside their institutions. Faculty in preservice teaching programs are involved in collaborations with K–12 schools on a regular basis as a result of student-teaching assignments and professional service for in-service programming (Shinners, 2006). When faculty members and K–12 schools work in collaboration to support preservice teachers, they often encounter challenges in the partnership that require moving past the rhetoric of collaborations to the reality of the work (Stephens and Boldt, 2004). Professional development schools are formal collaborations between universities and schools that focus on creating effective professional development plans for preservice teachers; the ultimate focus is to create sites of best practice for training and research (Dubetz, Lawrence, and Gningue, 2002). Relationship building is at the heart of the reality of the work. The cultures of higher education and K–12 systems differ, resulting in faculty members and teachers having different reward structures in place for their work contributions, different levels of control over their time, and different hierarchies in place. The clash of the cultures requires bridging the two environments for collaborations to flourish.

Another form of faculty collaboration occurs with business partners. Faculty members often provide consulting services to organizations and professional associations. Furthermore, businesses offer support for academic departments and individual faculty research. Industrial sponsorship of academic departments reinforces the notion of academic capitalism (Slaughter and Rhoades, 2004), but a research study by Mendoza and Berger (2008) noted that the academic culture was unaffected by business involvement and concluded that sponsorship was a viable option for supporting the quality of education for students. As differences exist in context among educational partners, so too do variations in context and influencing factors between academics and business.

Faculty members as collaborators represent a microperspective of collaborations and often serve as initial organizers of partnerships. Figure 5 highlights the key elements undergirding faculty collaborations. As noted in this section, the move from individual faculty work to collaborative work is embedded in disciplinary contexts. Thus, the motivation to collaborate may differ depending on the field of study. Support for faculty collaboration includes the building of relationships and trust and the creation of shared goals. As with other forms of partnerships, communication is critical to sustainability. Challenges that may unbalance the faculty collaboration include the pressures on faculty allocation of their time, how they are rewarded for the various aspects of their work (which is embedded in both disciplinary norms and institutional culture), and roles as they relate to academic hierarchy.

As faculty members contemplate collaborating with others, a number of critical questions should be addressed at the inception of the group process.

FIGURE 5
Faculty as Collaborators

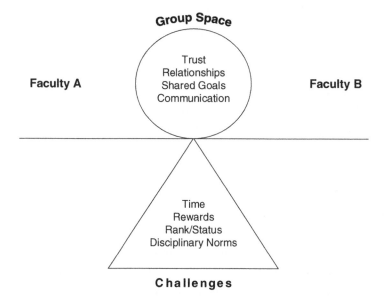

It is important to understand each group member's motivation for wanting to collaborate. For some faculty members, the motivation may be to have a support system on campus for the purposes of bouncing off and sharing ideas or reviewing manuscripts in progress. For other members, the needs may be more tangible in desiring a publication or seeking grant funding. Defining the goals of the collaborative effort also begins to provide structure to the relationships and to create shared meaning of what is desired. One partner may indicate that a goal is to have a support system in place and mean they want to have a social outlet, whereas another member may indicate the same desire for a support system but may assume it means others will edit manuscripts and provide connections in the discipline. Thus, having a clear understanding of basic elements is important.

Collaborators as Champions

Faculty collaborators often serve as the champion for institutional partnerships. Cooper and Mitsunaga (2010) found that faculty members were the initial champions in the partnerships they studied. They noted distinctions among faculty collaborations at the individual level, course level, and program level. An individual collaboration aligns with traditional definitions of faculty collaborations (Austin and Baldwin, 1991) in which a faculty member works with another faculty or an organization on a project. A move to the course level involves integration of two or more faculty in a teaching environment. In Cooper and Mitsunaga's research, this course collaboration occurred internationally rather than in a single university (Amey and Brown, 2004). Interdisciplinary collaborations around teaching (Holley, 2009) often provide a fertile environment for creating relationships that involve more parts of the university. Program collaboration meets the definition of partnerships put forth in this volume, as it involves two institutions working on a joint initiative. Increasingly, joint degree programs and collaborations are offered in international settings (Bologna Declaration, 1999; Cooper and Mitsunaga, 2010).

Faculty members who act as linchpins in collaborations often experience role strain (Boardman and Bozeman, 2007). In this case, faculty members have multiple allegiances—to their home institutions, to their collaborators, and to the partnership. They are simultaneously working on multiple projects with different supervisors and hold different roles in all these endeavors. Faculty members are socialized for their roles during their time in graduate school (Austin, 2002); thus, the faculty role models present in research institutions have a large impact on the professions and on how new faculty members anticipate their roles. New faculty face a number of different stresses as they assume tenure line positions (O'Meara, Terosky, and Neumann, 2009). Past research on initial role transitions highlights a number of different sources of stress and support (Eddy and Gayle, 2008; Sorcinelli, 2000); however, little research exists that discusses the added strain to faculty work that stretches roles to now include institutional collaborations.

Role shifts are most often researched in moves from faculty to administration (Gmelch and Parkay, 1999) and focus on different types of work required as an administrator rather than a scholar. Faculty champions often take on similar administrative roles as they work to form partnerships. One difficulty in this case is the lack of experience with administrative oversight and a lack of recognition of this type of work in the traditional tenure and promotion cycle. Despite these challenges, it is often faculty members who serve on the front line as initiators of partnerships.

Recently, Amey (2010) investigated a number of international partnerships under way and determined that each was started as the result of an individual faculty member's interest and involvement. Amey points out several challenges in this mode of partnership development. First, the partnership is vested in the role of the faculty champion: thus, uncertainty exists about the sustainability of the partnership should the champion's involvement stop. Second, the partnerships generated from the interests of the faculty member occur in the larger context of the department and by default affect resource allocation and time commitments beyond the individual champion. Finally, faculty members are not rewarded for their partnership work per se, only for the products of their efforts. Thus, individual champions might serve as an important catalyst for a developing partnership, but at some point, institutional commitment is required.

Location on the bottom of the organizational hierarchy provides faculty champions with a great deal of autonomy with regard to positional power (Morgan, 2006). In this capacity, faculty members have distinct networks and see institutional challenges differently. Faculty members collaborate to get things done (Lattuca and Creamer, 2005). Faculty members have flexibility in their positions to structure their time and projects. From this perspective, they have a certain level of power for flying below the radar, which allows time for projects to be nurtured and to grow before becoming institutionalized. This form of loose coupling (Weick, 1976) provides flexibility not available when institutions take on formalized programs.

Supports

As with all champions, faculty champions have certain types of power at their disposal. Faculty members have expertise that gives them a base of power. Their disciplinary orientation provides links with others, creating a network upon which collaborations can be built. Faculty members also build up alliances through their professional associations; these positions provide experience in bringing others together and background for administrative leadership. Faculty members enter into academics to follow their passion (Neumann,

2009); this passion often provides the charismatic spark to motivate others to join a project. Faculty members possess power in their informal systems of operation in institutions.

For networking, faculty members can act as the node to connect disparate networks. As Granovetter (1983) noted, it is often these types of weak ties that help create the types of networks required to make partnerships succeed, as they bring together individuals outside the limited range of a tight network. In the faculty, individuals have ties not only to those in the college community and in their professional and social networks but also with various community stakeholders. Faculty links with alumni provide additional connections. The number of links allows faculty champions more options to connect than formal leaders have at their disposal.

The advantage of faculty champions' lack of formal authority is that they operate in a loosely coupled context (Weick, 1976). Loose coupling allows for perseverance of identity at the same time partners are able to link. It is the weak ties that allow for testing the ideas and concepts inherent in partnerships, as they allow for localized adaptation. The ability to operate in informal networks allows faculty champions an opportunity to build networks not always possible through more formal routes. Leaders can take advantage of these opportunities to foster a number of possible ventures and then support those that take root.

Another lever of power that individual faculty have at their disposal is the power of leading upward. Useem (2003) presents examples of organizational members lower on the organizational hierarchy being able to exert their influence upward. Forms of shared leadership and leadership throughout the organization (Peterson, 1998) provide additional opportunities for faculty to exert their leadership in an institution. Faculty may be able to advocate to partnerships in which they are involved and find means to institutionalize the partnership for longer-term effect.

Challenges

Several challenges exist for faculty champions. First, partnerships often become invested in the individual faculty member and cannot be sustained when the initial champion is not present (Amey, 2010). The advantages that a faculty member brings to the development of a partnership serve as a double-edged benefit, as the personal connections that serve in the initial phases may become a deterrent when the faculty champion is no longer available.

Faculty members have a variety of roles, and the time required by the partnership may become too onerous and other projects take precedence. The elimination of the faculty as the bridge for the various partners may eliminate the node in the network that holds the collaboration together. Without a reward structure in place that recognizes the roles in the partnership, the benefits may not be great enough for continued participation. Additionally, faculty members may change institutions. Institutional shifts alter the organizational capital committed to partnerships. Whether the partnership moves with the champion to the new institution or remains at the old institution is questionable.

Faculty mobility provides just one threat against the institutionalization of partnerships. Other demands in the college may require institutional resources; the very nature of the loose coupling that served so well in the development of the partnership does not support institutionalization. The transition to a tightly coupled system with predictable outcomes requires the integration of the partnership into the organizational culture and policies. It is often beyond the power of a faculty champion to ensure changes in college policy or to leverage enough power to formally institutionalize a partnership.

Conclusion

Faculty champions serve a critical role in the formation of partnerships. They are able to provide the ground-level work required to bring partners together and can use their influence at their home institutions to obtain organizational capital. It is important for academic leaders to recognize these important contributions and work them into the reward system by adjusting policy to recognize these efforts. Creating incubator spaces for these initiatives to operate—and space to fail—is important.

Professional disciplines in colleges can provide useful networking opportunities. These schools serve to provide support for community partners, including educational institutions, businesses, and policymakers. The outreach functions of these disciplines create the type of links that provide fertile grounds for the creation of partnerships. Individual faculty can use these networks to build upon these connections.

Future Issues

THE CHALLENGES FACING HIGHER EDUCATION are hard to ignore. Cuts in resources for institutions and the increased demand for interdisciplinary work to solve the grand challenges of higher education create pressure for institutions and faculty to collaborate. Preparing for the future requires rethinking faculty work and institutional operations. Several key questions guide these planning efforts: How must faculty work be structured to reward expanded collaborative roles? How can institutional leaders create an environment to foster creative and innovative partnerships? How can organizational resources be used most effectively? What types of contexts best support collaborations?

This chapter reviews different motivations to partner and discusses how these types of motivations might affect the sustainability of future partnerships. An emerging form of collaboration is the creation of international partnerships. Europe has been building on the Bologna Declaration (1999) to help assert prominence in the area of higher education, though gains of the reform differ in each country, depending on conditions in each country (Oh, 2008). Accreditation thus provides a value-added benefit for universities meeting the stated criteria (Stensakera and Harvey, 2006) as U.S. institutions enter foreign higher education markets. This need for sanctioned programs has spurred U.S. colleges and universities to seek more international educational partnerships, particularly in the area of joint degree programs and expansions of historic study abroad programs. The call for students to have global competencies has also affected how U.S. institutions view curricular requirements as students become global citizens (Ewell, 2004). Crucial to all this need are issues that include the centrality of collaborations to the institution's mission, funding structures, and best ways to get it all done.

As institutions plan ahead, they might consider several suggestions presented here to aid planning. The concept of strategic partnerships is central to the health and well-being of institutions of higher education. Strategic initiatives help to build capacity for the larger group and the home institution and can leverage change for mutual gains. Several references provide a broad overview of the research on partnerships that may be of value.

Economics Versus Altruism

The early part of this volume reviewed various motivations for partnering. Two distinct types of motivations may drive the formation of collaborations and higher education policies. On the one hand, partners may seek to collaborate based on economic factors—seeking to share facilities, increase efficiencies, and save resources that all affect the bottom line. On the other hand, partners may desire to collaborate to achieve a shared goal or vision—creating a more altruistic rationale for partnering. In this case, common goals might include improved student learning, advances in an interdisciplinary area of work, or collaboration to support regional initiatives.

Economic motivations can serve to meet business and development needs. Griffin and Curtin (2007) found that partnerships based on vocational education and training served a key role in facilitating regional economic development. Partners were driven by the financial gains they all accrued. What remains unknown in this case is how long the partnership will continue once the economic goals have been met. The extrinsic motivation of financial gain provides only a limited push to keep partnerships together. The influence of compliance is only achieved when the motivator is present (Kelman, 1961), in this case, when financial gain is available. Intrinsic motivations, on the other hand, may be longer lasting in that they are based on internal drivers and alignment with value systems (Kelman, 1961). For instance, a program involving colleges and local EcoVillages helped to create a sustainability curriculum on campuses (Allen-Gil and others, 2005) that developed as a result of shared goals rather than economic gains per se.

Policymakers clearly see partnerships as economic levers (Johnston and Noftsinger, 2004). The push for P–16 partnerships serves as a means for educational reform of the system but also aspires to create economic efficiencies. Collaboration across educational sectors provides a means to avoid duplicate services and to support students better for educational progress. It makes a difference, however, in how these goals are achieved—top down by mandates or bottom up with grass-roots support. National policymakers and funding agencies see educational partnerships as providing a platform for innovation and as a means to improve business development (see the American Recovery and Reinvestment Act of 2009). Additionally, a focus on the technology exchange from universities to practice provides one means to an end for partnerships.

The creation of consortia to pool resources and save costs is rooted in historical practice (Baus and Ramsbottom, 1999). More recently, however, the specter of mergers has become more prevalent as states and nations seek to find the best means to support higher education. Mergers differ from partnerships because they are often foisted on institutions and involve dissolution of the original college organizations. Research on a merger formed with a former federation of four universities in Australia determined that three strategies contributed to success: creation of an open communications channel, engagement of staff, and a supportive work environment (Sebalj, Hudson, Ryan, and Wight-Boycott, 2007). The combination of these features created a shared value system, standardized policies, and staff empowerment. But the gains were achieved only as a result of strong leadership in guiding the newly merged organization.

Beyond economic rationales for merging is the desire to create diverse opportunities. Lang (2003) argues that if diversification of programs and services is the end objective of mergers, different guidelines for choosing partners will be sought. According to Harmon and Harmon (2008), the move is away from the historic reasons for merging to address an institution's shortcomings to one based on strategic objectives. A case in point is the change under way in the Finnish higher education system (Tirronen and Nokkala, 2009). The researchers stress that the aim of the collaborations is to increase the competitiveness of Finnish universities. They used three forms of structural development: cooperation and mergers of institutions, differences in niche advantages, and changes in governance and leadership. The push toward mergers in this case is to create a system built on the best of the current system of colleges rather than thinking of it as a deficit model that requires fixing.

A prime example of the use of policy to promote educational partnerships is the Bologna Declaration (1999). Grek and Lawn (2009) note that a common element in efforts toward Europeanization was the creation of a common identity, with a core contributing factor focusing on education. "The shift toward a 'Europe of Knowledge' in the late 1990s involved a further intensification of the early work on collaboration, network, symbolic acts, and the systematization of the vocational and higher education arena" (Grek and Lawn, 2009, p. 34). The focus recently turned to outputs, in particular the development of common student learning outcomes. Underscoring this goal was recognition of heightened student mobility, which could be supported and enhanced by ease of transfer among colleges and universities.

Furthermore, Grek and Lawn (2009) noted that "apart from establishing new strategic goals and the policy frameworks to push them, the Lisbon European Council was significant for one more reason: it was the first time that the Council promoted the need for European education systems to converge" (p. 37). European systems and those in other countries developing and expanding their higher education systems (for example, China and India) have the advantage of centralized systems overseeing institutions of higher education. The United States lacks this type of centralized form of policymaking in higher education. Instead, individual states are responsible for oversight of the systems located in their boundaries.

The Spellings Report (U.S. Department of Education, 2006) attempted to provide a framework of accountability to ensure outcomes from the country's higher education institutions. The report pointed out the misalignment between public schools and institutions of higher education as one factor hindering the continuing of a world-class educational system in the United States. The commissioners outlined six areas of focus: access, cost and affordability, financial aid, learning, transparency and accountability, and innovation. Despite the national calls for changes in higher education, no consensus was achieved on approach and no guiding policy created. Instead, policy changes regarding systematic coordination of higher education remain in the purview of individual states.

Individual states bear a mantle of responsibility for the future. A collaborative formed by the Education Commission of the States, the National Center for Higher Education Management Systems, and the National Center for Public Policy and Higher Education sought to help states improve their systems of higher education and establish priorities for improvement. The guide created by the collaborative put forth five steps to set a public agenda:

1. Appoint a leadership group;
2. Ground the agenda and its priorities in the needs of the state residents;
3. Complete a higher education policy audit;
4. Meet with key people throughout the state;
5. Report back to the leadership group, finalize the public agenda, and assign responsibilities [Davies, 2006, p. 9].

As the policy collaborative investigated best practices in place, it identified a number of lessons:

Setting a public agenda for higher education requires sustained leadership.
Data analysis is a critical first step.
Policy issues overlap and extend beyond higher education.
The face of America is changing.
Every state needs its own policy agenda.
State relationships with higher education are shifting.
Performance incentives in the state budget have to align with the public agenda (Davies, 2006, pp. 10–17).

These lessons show the interconnections between institutions of higher education and other challenges facing states. Changing demographics present new pressures on states that differ by state location and, ultimately, needs of stakeholders. Assessment of policies is required to show any effects individual policies may have on other policies. Instead of viewing colleges and universities with an institution-centered approach, states must confront this fragmented approach to higher education, which may be counterproductive to state needs. As it does on an institutional basis, budget support must align with policy decisions (Fowler, 2009). These strategies require a break from the historical organization and governance of higher education by states.

An important element of sustaining partnerships is shared values. Billett, Ovens, Clemans, and Seddon (2007) investigated ten long-serving social partnerships. Like other research on successful partnerships, this research pointed out a series of crucial central principles and practices, namely, shared goals, relations with partners, capacity for partnership work, governance and leadership, and trust and trustworthiness. Notably, the rationale for sustainability was not economic, though benefits did accrue. As this research shows, the links between economic and value-driven partnerships are not totally separate. Universities can serve as change agents for regions based on the value of commitment to supporting educational goals, but at the same time, these initiatives can improve the area economically (Welty and Lukens, 2009).

Dickie and Dickie (2009) examined current research on educational partnerships in Southeast Asia using a three-round Delphi technique to weigh the pros and cons of partnerships. They determined that mutual benefits were evident when a conceptual framework was based on expectations and principals of partners. Policymakers can serve as a driving force, but it is necessary to have trusted partnerships at the local level as building blocks (Chang and Cha, 2008). The presence of shared values thus provides a better foundation to meet goals. Serving mutual interests is aided by frequent, open communication. Johnston and Noftsinger (2004) determined that articulated goals require long-term objectives; thus, short-term reciprocity should be deemphasized. Time is required to change systems of operation and to obtain outcomes, but the tendency in partnerships is to look for the quick fix and immediate gains (Eddy, 2007). When shared values are present, partners are better equipped to weather the rough patches, because group members trust that ultimate gains will be achieved over time.

Setting a public agenda in higher education includes both economic and altruistic rationales. On the one hand, economics serves as a strong lever to guide policy and push institutions toward collaborations. On the other hand, the values and vision of each state establish the framework of goals. Harris (2005) argues that the dominant form of partnerships that promote a modern agenda is instrumentalist and economically driven. She points out that this approach limits the potential of collaborations and instead makes the case for conceptualizing partnerships as learning partnerships in which collaboration would be shared. The creation of shared goals is at the heart of long-standing collaborations. As states and the colleges in them navigate to the future, both economic and altruistic motives will drive them forward. Even though economics may provide the initial push for partnering, collaborators must develop a shared vision for the group for long-term success.

Partnerships Across Educational Borders

International partnerships add another layer to the formation and development of partnerships. The expansion of the global market and opening of borders formerly closed to the United States provide a number of opportunities for partnering. Despite this potential, recent research reports that U.S. faculty members are less involved with international efforts (Finkelstein, Walker, and Chen, 2009). Those authors determined that U.S. faculty lagged well behind their international counterparts with respect to faculty work involving collaboration with international scholars, research that was international in scope, publishing in foreign counties, or teaching courses with an emphasis on international content. Contributing to less international involvement is limited faculty mobility (O'Hara, 2009). Sabbatical leaves serve as one means to travel abroad for extended periods of time but require a certain level of seniority and institutional support, not to mention family flexibility if faculty members' partners or children are involved. Sabbatical leaves are often on the budget chopping block as university funding decreases. Obtaining funding for foreign travel is also challenging, with programs such as the Fulbright Scholar Program providing one source of funds for U.S. scholars (see http://www.cies .org/). Additionally, the European Union–United States Atlantis Program funds projects that help develop transatlantic curricula and support structures for undergraduate students (see http://www.ed.gov/programs/fipseec/ index.html).

Colleges and universities in the United States seek to partner internationally as a means to supplement revenue streams (Hodson and Thomas, 2001; Labi, 2009b; Zahn, Sandell, and Lindsay, 2007). International partnerships may occur on a variety of levels and include different stakeholders. For instance, partnerships may be established to afford students or faculty study-abroad experiences, to establish a venue for knowledge sharing, to develop joint curricula, or to develop academic and business partnerships (Turner and Robson, 2008). Like domestic partnerships, international partnerships are formed to generate mutual benefits for the partners (Tedrow and Mabokela, 2007).

Initial forays into international collaborations may begin with the work of a single faculty member (Amey, 2010; Cooper and Mitsunaga, 2010). For example, South Korea hopes to lure partners, given its location and the chance to get in on the ground floor of entrepreneurial opportunities. For their part, however, U.S. colleges are adopting a cautious approach, beginning first by expanding faculty collaborations and sending students to study in South Korea, with a focus on graduate programs and on forming research alliances with high-tech companies (Fischer, 2009). Less commitment is required when operating collaborations that focus on individuals rather than institutions, which may require more formal memorandums of understanding.

More formal ventures of offering joint educational programs or degrees involve higher levels of institutional commitment. Policymakers look to universities to partner with others to aid in globalization efforts (Hay and Kapitzke, 2009). Holland (2010) reported on the efforts of a Canadian community college to offer degree programs in China, emphasizing the need to have shared meaning in the memorandum of understanding and the importance of building and keeping relationships over time. Differences in culture are a source of misunderstanding in international collaborations that can contribute to a lack of trust and ultimately to a lack of commitment to the partnership (Tedrow and Mabokela, 2007).

As with domestic partnerships, several key features contribute to successful joint ventures. Heffernan and Poole (2005) found that clear communication of expectations, trust generated by time spent working together and understanding partners' strengths, and obvious commitment to the project were critical to partnerships' viability. Further, it is important to pay attention to the detailed work of the collaboration, including agreements on funding disbursements and obligations, contractual obligations, the timing of academic calendars and course delivery, and common understanding of underlying value systems rooted in cultural differences (Tedrow and Mabokela, 2007). In attempts to improve science and math education in Indonesia, for instance, joint planning times helped focus on developing similar program goals, ultimately resulting in the creation of collegiality and partnership capital (Saito, Imansyah, Kubok, and Hendayana, 2007).

Relationship building is central to the creation of international partnerships, but distance and time differences create challenges in developing these budding associations. The use of technology begins to bridge these challenges and provides a cost-effective means for developing connections. Willis (2008) focused on the role of relationships in partnerships and found they are central to successful alliances. Critical to Chinese partnerships is the development of *guanxi,* the deep, personal relationships between individuals required to do business (Willis, 2008, p. 223). In exploring the nature of the *guanxi* connections, Willis (2008) identified three types of relationships: basic friends, working colleagues, and neutral relationships. Basic friends had a simplistic relationship that is cordial but more superficial, working colleagues were formed on a simple level but involved colleagues from China and abroad, and neutral relationships negated any form of relationship and were often used to establish a response to rude behavior or insults. *Guanxi* relationships, on the other hand, were the "cement" between the two foreign partners and were built on honesty, reciprocity, empathy, and trust (p. 228). These types of relationships developed at different stages—personal, social, professional, and organizational. As individuals garner social capital because of these relationships, organizational connections follow that help support successful alliances. It was through the development of more mature friendships that honest and open dialogue could occur that truly advanced the partnership.

Willis (2008) also found a range of organizational relationships: formal, informal, and hidden. Formal relationships provided the framework for the alliance, often occurring with key individuals from both partnerships. Informal relationships, on the other hand, were not recognizable on an organizational chart but were happenstance connections among individuals from both partner organizations. On the other hand, hidden organizational relationships were found most often among Chinese partners and represented deep *guanxi* relationships based on power. To keep operations running smoothly, however, required a range of relationships rather than only one type.

The various levels of personal relationships outlined above underscore the time required to develop successful international partnerships. The context in which the partnerships develop goes beyond the individuals involved. Patterson's research (2005) on the General Agreement on Trade in Services found processes in place relative to each individual country's need to protect its own tertiary educational system. Tensions were evident when national collaborative goals ran counter to competitive or supranational policy. As in domestic partnerships, the power of individual partners influences the alliance.

Cross-border collaborations often privilege one partner over another based on which partner is perceived to hold more power, based on knowledge, resources, control over processes, or ties to governmental approval agencies. Maldonado-Maldonada and Cantwell (2008) determined that despite these administrative rationales, the insecurities and desires of the individual collaborators played a more prominent role in cross-border academic work, even though it was embedded in the larger contexts of the countries. Thus, the role of the champion is critical in navigating these types of international endeavors. As Willis (2008) found, individual partner connections create the environment of trust required for successful collaborations.

Brewer (2010) reported on the necessity for faculty buy-in to help internationalize the curriculum and to build study abroad programs beneficial to students. She further noted that faculty development programs at the home institution were a critical source of support for international efforts. Faculty exchange programs provided an opportunity for faculty members to learn about other countries and to create opportunities that bridged this experience with the classroom context.

Increasingly, developing countries have turned to U.S. colleges and universities for help in developing their programs of higher education (Altbach, Reisberg, and Rumbley, 2009), because the United States has the most recognized university system in the world (Shanghai Jiao Tong University, 2009). Rankings have taken on heightened importance as foreign countries develop their systems of higher education (Hazelkorn, 2009). Partnering with U.S. institutions (Labi, 2009a) provides developing countries cachet and a chance to leverage U.S. experience. Hvistendahl (2009) reported how Chinese academics benefited from American academic collaborations, allowing China to quickly gain expertise and the American academics to gain valuable research opportunities. International partnerships set up for mutual gain proved most successful.

Numerous pathways and options exist for international partnerships. The American Council on Education recently studied thirty-one institutions to determine plans for internationalization (Childress, 2009). Internationalization might include partnerships with foreign counties but could also include domestic plans to expand the curriculum to have a global focus. The council found a number of universities with specific plans regarding their global efforts. The study identified five benefits and functions of internationalization plans; an internationalization plan serves as a:

Roadmap for internationalization
Vehicle to develop buy-in
Mechanism for explain the meaning and goals of internationalization
Medium for interdisciplinary collaboration, and
Tool for fundraising.

A formalized plan provides multiple purposes. First, a plan communicates to stakeholders the areas of focus for the university and how the university plans to achieve its goals. Second, it serves a symbolic role because it communicates to potential partners its commitment to international ventures. Finally, the process involved in creating the plan allows opportunity for open communication to help articulate the value system and visionary goals important to the university, which provides an additional element of organizational capital as resources are devoted to these efforts.

Partnerships that cross national borders will become increasingly more common in the future. Other countries are increasing their financial commitment to develop their systems of higher education, at just the time when state support for public education in the United States is diminishing (Labi, 2009b). U.S. colleges and universities seek international partnerships for a variety of reasons, including to supplement revenue streams, to internationalize the curriculum and help students learn global competencies, to leverage faculty research, and to build university-business joint ventures in emerging markets. Despite the motivation to enter international markets, not all university ventures have succeeded (Kolowich, 2009), thus making it crucial to consider what is most important when seeking international partners. The research reviewed in this section underscores the importance of relationship building for successful partnerships (Willis, 2008). Faculty members often serve as the building blocks for these partnerships, as they are initially involved on a more personal scale doing research, working on joint curricula, or overseeing student study abroad programs (Amey, 2010; Brewer and Cunningham, 2010). In international partnerships in particular, time is required to develop the type of deep relationships required for successful ventures. Time allows for overcoming initial language and cultural barriers and creating shared partnership goals.

Planning Ahead

This volume has reviewed a variety of forms of partnerships and outlined a number of elements that can help support these ventures as well as challenges that might diminish them. Several key features are apparent for those contemplating partnerships as well as different levels of involvement to consider in forming and developing partnerships. Individual champions serve a critical role in promoting partnerships and using their social networks to bring individuals together. Second, institutional leaders play a crucial role in creating buy-in for the partnership (Kotter and Cohen, 2002). Top-level buy-in is important, because it opens access to organizational capital in the institution. Finally, the organizational framework and context create the backdrop against which partnerships grow or flounder. Understanding organizational operations can provide insight into the types of levers most appropriate to support partnerships.

Three areas are singled out for planning ahead. The first concerns environmental scanning. It is important to understand both the external environment in which the partnership will occur and how the internal operations can best support the arrangements. Second, as indicated throughout this volume, relationships provide crucial support to budding collaborations. Evaluating the social networks in place can provide leverage in the developing stages. Finally, the creation of communication pathways and the framing of the partnership contribute to how others perceive the joint efforts.

Environmental Scanning

Understanding the challenges facing colleges and universities is the first step in establishing the advantages and disadvantages of partnering (Davies, 2006). Environmental scanning involves gathering various forms of data to analyze and determining the best strategic tactics available. Colleges and universities have borrowed from business practices (Birnbaum, 2000), including a S-W-O-T analysis to outline strengths, weaknesses, opportunities, and threats or a P-E-S-T analysis to consider political, economical, social, and technological contexts.

The types and levels of scans depend on the position of the partner. For individual champions, determinations of whether to partner or not are often rooted in the depth of the relationship with the potential partner. The depth of relationships is based on the extent of social networks, the level of trust established between individuals, and the motivations of each partner. Champions enter into collaborations to accomplish individual goals, often based on research interests, a desire to advance student learning, and a desire to support institutional objectives. Determination of partnering involves less risk on an individual level, as the investment is often less and more limited to time and individual resources.

Institutional leadership is critical to change initiatives (Davies, 2006; Kotter and Cohen, 2002). As leaders create plans, they rely on data to determine the most pressing needs facing their institutions and how best to address these issues. Data-driven decision making is critical in defining the landscape in which collaborations occur. Understanding how partners can help meet strategic goals is an important consideration for college leaders. It is also important for leaders to understand the organizational capital that can be committed to partnerships. Likewise, it is important to develop memorandums of understanding that outline the use of resources, define roles, and establish goals.

Organizational frameworks affect the ways in which data are acquired and interpreted. In a structural frame, rational decision making considers all options before determining a plan of action. In a human resource frame, the most central data affect human resources, whereas in a political frame, the formation of a dominant coalition guides decision making. Finally, in the symbolic frame, decisions are made that most align with the underlying culture and value system in place.

Building Relationships

Key to the success of a partnership is building relationships (Baus and Ramsbottom, 1999; Heffernan and Poole, 2005). Relationships are first built by individuals and then shift to institutions. Individual faculty champions build connections through their disciplinary associations and in their community engagement. As these networks develop, trust is built over time. The centrality of the champion to the issue and the density of the relationship influence the development of social networks (Coleman, 1988; Granovetter, 1983; Scott, 1988). Additionally, interactions with others connect individuals to broader social networks beyond their own that provide the range of ties outlined by Granovetter (1983) that best support collaborations. It is through these multiple levels of connections that larger networks are created. As noted, however, higher education institutions looking to build community engagement need to craft a shift in how faculty involvement is rewarded (Saltmarsh, Giles, Ward, and Buglione, 2009). When faculty champions are rewarded for their work in creating partnerships, more possibilities for collaboration are created.

Leaders play a critical role in building relationships as well. A central component of change models is the creation of coalitions (Kotter and Cohen, 2002); leaders influence the culture of an institution regarding the ways in which relationships are valued (Morgan, 2006). Institutions operating in a human resources frame place a premium on relationships, whereas the shifting nature of coalitions in a political orientation indicates that the value of the relationship depends on the issue at hand. Leadership that is facilitative or inclusive (Amey and Brown, 2004) fosters relationship building that aligns with individuals' internal value systems (Kelman, 1961) and ultimately creates a more transformational environment (Burns, 1978).

State leaders and policymakers also have a role in relationship building. When stakeholders are involved in the creation of state educational goals and objectives, they are more likely to buy in to policies that require collaboration. State coordinating bodies and statewide associations for college personnel begin to create networks that foster the exchange of ideas and establish links for those involved. The more networks established in a region or state, the more possibilities exist for potential linking of institutions, businesses, and associations.

Framing the Partnership

Communication is a key component in successful partnerships (Baus and Ramsbottom, 1999; Heffernan and Poole, 2005; Sebalj, Hudson, Ryan, and Wight-Boycott, 2007). The creation of shared meaning contributes to the ways in which partnership stakeholders conceptualize the partnerships and how they see the longer-term objectives (Weick, 1995). Framing the partnership occurs at multiple levels (Fairhurst and Sarr, 1996). Pick (2003) researched a college merger using a frame perspective and found that competing interpretations affected how the merger occurred. The author used three frames of analysis borrowed from Schön and Rein (1994): rhetorical frames, action frames, and positional frames. Rhetorical frames refers to the underlying interpretation of a policy issue and outlines the general story and value system for institutional members. Action frames cover the level of commitment to a particular course of action, whereas positional frames link to specific interpretations that resonate with the stakeholder institution (p. 302). The frame analysis concluded that the various framing perspectives competed to shape interpretations.

Pick (2003) found that the rhetorical frames in place highlighted the underlying cultural values of the partners and that this process allowed for a recasting of interpretation of events from a local level to a platform situated in global competitiveness; this change resulted in a key frame shift of understanding. The level of commitment to the merger shifted over time as internal alliances were formed. Ultimately, positions and understandings were influenced by various policy reports and media reporting on the merger process (Fowler, 2009). The use of framing by individual institutional leaders and policymakers affected how the merger was accomplished, underscoring this key element in planning for partnerships.

Fairhurst and Sarr (1996) outlined the role of framing as a tactic for leaders to call attention to particular events and actions. In this case, the first step is for individuals to discern key meanings for themselves before setting the frame of view for others (Weick, 1995). Multiple options exist for perspectives to offer to campus members; thus, the chosen perspective serves as a guide for the meaning attributed to the partnership. Given that research has concluded that shared values are an important pillar for creating partnerships, leaders should frame collaborations in a fashion that links them to the college's core value system. Likewise, faculty champions will find more support for their efforts when they communicate them in ways that show how the partnership aligns with the vision of the college.

The institutional frame provides the context in which partnerships develop and is the public persona that potential partners observe. The college vision, however, does not occur in a vacuum and is influenced by external factors. As change occurs, shifts in the value system may occur (Pick, 2003) and result in a reinterpretation of institutional needs and hence ways in which collaborations are viewed. Leaders have a great deal of control over the interpretations others have of situations (Eddy, 2003; Neumann, 1995) and in this capacity can target stakeholders' attention to particular meanings. Framing is ongoing and is reinforced by rituals, jargon, and institutional stories (Clark, 1972; Fairhurst and Sarr, 1996; Weick, 1995). How the partnership is portrayed to stakeholders provides an essential role in the partnership's ultimate success.

Strategic Partnerships

Partnerships will become increasingly important as challenges build for institutions of higher education. Colleges and universities face a broad array of possible partnering opportunities. This monograph provided examples of various sources of motivation for partnering and contexts in which partnerships occur. The motivation to partner to save resources or for economic development brings economic benefits to the forefront in developing partnerships. As evident, partnerships driven on pure economic gain are destined to fail once the financial incentives are no longer available (Eddy, 2007). Partnerships based on reform efforts emerging from shared values such as seeking to improve student learning, on the other hand, intend to bring about change

FIGURE 6
Strategic Partnerships

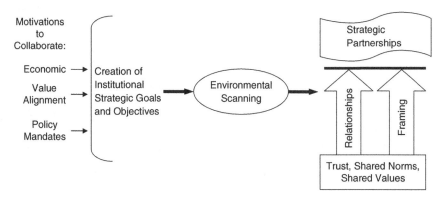

to the current educational system through the leverage of partnerships. Finally, partnerships based on shared visions or goals create a synergy and buy-in for participants that help cement relationships and build trust in seeking common desires. Each form of partnerships may meet an institution's strategic goal but does so differently.

Strategic collaborations are needed in the future. Strategic partnerships differ from the unplanned collaborations of the past, because they are entered into to meet institutional strategic goals and to build institutional capacity (Zeelen and van der Linden, 2009). The examples throughout this volume underscore the typical happenstance nature of partnership formation versus intentional planning to build particular types of partnerships. Various champions serve to promote the final partnerships developed, which often occur based on an individual faculty member's or campus member's personal involvement with a project, research, or requests by community members or international parties. Figure 6 presents a model for strategic partnerships that includes the elements outlined in this section.

The model highlights how a number of motivating forces exist for the creation of partnerships. A critical component for the creation of strategic partnerships is for each institution to have evaluated its core values, goals, and objectives. Partners can then be sought through environmental scanning to find collaborators whose goals align best with the vision of the college. Central pillars of the partnership are relationships and framing approaches. Relationships are built on trust and shared values. Framing involves a variety of communication venues that articulate what is central for the partners and aids in providing interpretation for campus stakeholders. Ultimately, the creation of partnership capital is possible when the partners share norms and goals for the collaboration.

As in other areas of partnering, strategic partnerships involve a number of levels in their formation. First, state policymakers must look to develop a systems perspective as they provide opportunities for higher education within their borders. Instead, colleges and universities must look to internal strategic planning initiatives to not only save resources (Van de Water and Rainwater, 2001) but also to view higher education systematically and evaluate the system based on state needs (Davies, 2006). Multiple stakeholders should have input into the process of creating the state educational agenda. An outcome of this evaluation process may include a restructuring of the higher education system and the development of partnerships to support the overall state vision. Next, state funding should be targeted to reward institutions that meet the strategic objectives of the states. For instance, Kentucky was an early leader in aligning state resources with needs identified in the state (Davies, 2006). Aligning values with funding sends a clear message of priorities and provides support for the type of services in demand in the state.

Next, institutions must create strategic plans that acknowledge and value their historical missions but also take a hard look at how the college fulfills needs in the region and state. A clearer sense of an internal value system will occur once a college has created its strategic plan. With this plan in hand, institutional leaders and faculty members can seek partnerships that align best with the college's internal vision. The critical networks that provide connections for partnership formation will then be based from the very beginning on shared values that can contribute to long-term stability.

Finally, champions for partnerships can be intentional in how they seek links with others when their efforts are embedded in a larger strategically focused context. When institutions align their reward systems with their strategic vision, faculty members have a ready system to recognize and reward their collaborative efforts as early champions. It is through this alignment of the levels of the system that enhanced outcomes can be achieved.

Conclusion

The research on best practices covered in this volume will aid individual faculty, college leaders, and policymakers as they seek and form partnerships. As outlined in the overview, partnerships and collaborations begin as the result of a number of different motivations. The reasons for working together provide the foundation for the future success or failure of these joint ventures. When partnerships are based strictly on extrinsic motivations, either because of mandates or in seeking funding that requires collaboration, longer-term success depends on the building of relationships, trust, and, ultimately, shared values. The absence of these features makes it more likely that the partnership will fail when the mandate shifts or the funding is gone (Eddy, 2007). When partnerships are the result of long-standing relationships or shared goals, the basis for cooperation is stronger. Jie (2010) used game theory to describe interactions and cooperation in a Sino–U.S. partnership between two universities. Game theory relies on the players' choice of self-interest or cooperative interests. When the former is greater, players (in this case colleges) seek to make decisions that benefit their self-interests over those of the partnership. This type of choice eventually results in the dissolution of the partnership.

This volume has highlighted a number of different examples of partnerships and the various factors that helped to make them successful. At the root of long-standing partnerships are relationships. Willis (2008) presents the idea of *guanxi,* the Chinese concept of deep personal relationships between individuals, to discuss how some partnerships obtain longevity. Trusting relationships emerge when collaborators have had time to work together, have been successful in obtaining some of their objectives, and have felt that their needs have been met and their contributions valued. Trust takes time to build.

The context in which collaborations emerge provides another critical aspect for partnerships, in particular those based on cross-border ventures. Understanding the culture from which the individual collaborators operate helps avoid misunderstandings. Obvious examples of language and cultural understanding are more apparent when dealing with different countries, but cultural differences exist even within borders. For instance, when a four-year university partners with a community college, the differences in mission, student demographics, or reward structures may result in partners having different meanings for student success. It is important to discuss the assumptions each partner brings to the venture and to develop a shared understanding of meaning of terms, objectives, and values. Ultimately, the creation of a shared value system is key to long-term sustainability.

A number of different practices can support joint ventures. Supports differ depending on the level of the collaborator (individual faculty, college leader, or policymaker). Each group needs to address different questions before becoming involved in a collaboration. The following paragraphs review each partner area and begin to provide a road map to follow in the consideration of whether or not to partner.

Faculty collaborators. Individuals are at the core of collaborations and partnerships, with initial faculty collaborations based on shared research interests or goals often providing the seed for institutional partnerships. As Austin and Baldwin (1991) concluded, key considerations exist for faculty as collaborators. They noted several initial questions for faculty to address before collaborating, including the choice of collaborators, the division of work, the creation of operating guidelines, and the objectives of the collaboration. Hinck and others (2009) found that faculty collaborators require the creation of a group space, which is produced over time based on the emergence of trust in the group.

Faculty members need to reflect on their own objectives for wanting to collaborate with others. Lattuca and Creamer (2005) point to the simple reason that faculty collaborate—to get things done. Each faculty member brings to the collaboration various levels of social capital, and ultimately this form of capital translates to different levels of power. It is important for faculty collaborators to acknowledge power differentials and discuss how they affect the relationship. Faculty with high levels of social capital are key champions for joint ventures, but it is important to move beyond a collaboration being so vested in an individual. If the partnership does not move beyond the individual, it is destined for failure once the person leaves.

Often, faculty collaborations evolve as the result of happenstance more than intentionality. Shared research interests, development of professional relationships over time, or committee work provide first points of connection and foster cooperation among individuals working together. As partnerships become more strategic, and because faculty work is expanding, it will become important for faculty to be selective in their involvement in various types of collaboration (Neumann, 2009).

Institutional leaders. Successful partnerships require buy-in from institutional leaders (Kotter and Cohen, 2002). Leaders can become more proactive by defining institutional goals that reward collaborative efforts. Creating small institutional grants to support interdisciplinary faculty collaborations can be a first step. The building of this group space may allow for creative generation of ideas for partnerships that can be scaled up to the institutional level. Likewise, the group space allows for a safe environment in which faculty may take risks and where failure is not cause for penalties. Here, too, disciplinary norms and expectations have an effect on how these teams are operationalized.

As faculty are pressed to work more collaboratively, both in institutions and with partners, it is crucial to align faculty reward structures to reflect the value of collaborative work (Creamer, 2005). College leaders may need to reassess tenure and promotion policies and design categories of scholarship that acknowledge the time-consuming nature of partnerships (Boyer, 1990). In particular, the initial stages of partnership formation are time consuming, and outcomes may not be evident until several years have elapsed.

Another key area that college leaders need to pay attention to is how they frame the role of partnerships in their institution's overall strategic mission (Neumann, 1995). How partnerships are talked about and presented to both internal and external audiences matters (Eddy, 2003). Various forms of communication will begin to create the portrait of the partnership and help stakeholders understand better the relative importance for the institution. Ultimately, the creation of shared meaning among partners about what the partnership is and what it hopes to accomplish contributes to long-term success. Leaders serve an important role in framing this shared meaning. Finally, leaders are typically involved in crafting memorandums of understanding for partnerships. Including as much clarity as possible in the memorandum regarding roles, partner contributions, deadlines, assessment points and evaluation, and partnership goals helps to eliminate points of contention.

Policymakers. Policymakers often look to partnerships and collaboration as a means to save resources and create efficiencies. As a result, mandates and policies often shape how interested partners assess participation with others in joint ventures. Merely dictating that parties need to work together, however, is not enough. Consideration needs to be given to what best supports partnerships and what helps move partnerships beyond one-time events to sustainable enterprises. As needs change over time, partnerships that are flexible are able to shift to meet new demands. This monograph has outlined several factors that contribute to successful partnerships.

Partnerships are built on relationships and trust. Policymakers can work to become more involved and invested in this arena. Building bridges to colleges and universities that connect theory and practice can result in the creation of policy based on data but also vested in state and national needs. Like institutional leaders, policymakers can help to frame meaning about what is meant when they indicate that collaborations are valued. Clarity in policy objectives and heightened transparency all contribute to building trust as well. Finally, continuity of policy creation and support helps move beyond one-time initiatives. Too often, the shifting political landscape results in changes in priorities and the discontinuation of support for previous collaborative work. This process reinforces collaborators looking to meet short-term goals rather than thinking of long-term solutions to the grand challenges facing education.

Policy writers need to recognize the levers at their disposal to initiate action. Clearly, the extrinsic motivations of regulations or funding provide important forces to bring partners together. Yet it is intrinsic motivators and commonly supported goals that are the cornerstone of a successful partnership. Understanding the human element involved and creating the space and time for partnerships to grow are important. The current stress on educational systems demands attention to the processes that will help support collaborative efforts to address these challenges.

Summary. Key supports for partnership development and sustainability include strong relationships nurtured over time, trust, frequent and open communication, shared values and vision, and a common understanding of what it means to be involved in the partnership. Constant evaluation of the collaborative efforts helps inform those involved so that adjustments can be made. The creation of a governance process establishes the framework required to support the partnership and the policies that oversee the ways in which feedback is obtained and future plans made. The challenges facing higher education require rethinking and reconceptualizing business as usual. Partnerships provide an answer for some of these challenges.

References

Acker, J. (1990). Hierarchies, jobs, bodies: A theory of gendered organizations. *Gender and Society, 4*(2), 139–158.

Adler, P. S., and Kwon, S. (2002). Social capital: Prospects for a new concept. *Academy of Management Review, 27*(1), 17–40.

Allen-Gil, S., and others. (2005). Forming a community partnership to enhance education in sustainability. *International Journal, 6*(4), 392–402.

Altbach, P. G. (1998). *Comparative higher education: Knowledge, the university, and development.* Greenwich, CN: Ablex.

Altbach, P. G., Reisberg, L., and Rumbley, L. (2009). *Trends in global higher education: Tracking an academic revolution.* Chestnut Hill, MA: Boston College Center for International Higher Education.

American Association of Colleges for Teacher Education. (2005). *Partnerships for success: No Child Left Behind meets the Higher Education Act.* Washington, DC: American Association of Colleges for Teacher Education.

American Association of State Colleges and Universities. (2004). *Crossing boundaries. The urban education imperative: A report from the joint task force for urban/metropolitan schools.* Washington, DC: American Association of State Colleges and Universities.

American Association of State Colleges and Universities. (2009). *Top 10 state policy issues for higher education in 2009.* Washington, DC: American Association of State Colleges and Universities.

Amey, M. J. (Ed.). (2007). *Collaborations across education sectors.* New Directions for Community Colleges, no. 139. San Francisco: Jossey-Bass.

Amey, M. J. (2010). Administrative perspectives on international partnerships. In P. L. Eddy (Ed.), *International collaborations: Institutional frameworks and faculty roles.* New Directions for Higher Education, no. 150. San Francisco: Jossey-Bass.

Amey, M. J., and Brown, D. F. (2004). *Breaking out of the box: Interdisciplinary collaboration and faculty work.* Boston: Information Age Publishing.

Amey, M. J., Eddy, P. L., Campbell, T., and Watson, J. (2008). *The role of social capital in facilitating partnerships.* Paper presented at the 2008 Council for the Study of Community Colleges annual conference, Philadelphia, PA.

Amey, M. J., Eddy, P. L., and Ozaki, C. K. (2007). Demands for partnerships and collaboration in higher education: A model. In M. J. Amey (Ed.), *Collaborations across educational borders.* New Directions for Community Colleges, no.139. San Francisco: Jossey-Bass.

Anderson, R. D., and Sundre, D. L. (2005). Assessment partnership: A model for collaboration between two-year and four-year institutions. *Assessment Update, 17*(5), 8.

Astin, A., and Astin, H. (2000). *Leadership reconsidered: Engaging higher education in social change.* Battle Creek, MI: W. K. Kellogg Foundation.

Austin, A. E. (2002). Preparing the next generation of faculty: Graduate school as socialization to the academic career. *Journal of Higher Education, 73,* 94–122.

Austin, A. E., and Baldwin, R. G. (1991). *Faculty collaboration: Enhancing the quality of scholarship and teaching.* ASHE-ERIC Higher Education Report, vol. 20, no. 7. Washington, DC: School of Education and Human Development, George Washington University.

Baker, G. A., III. (2002). American higher education at the Rubicon: A partnership for progress. *Community College Journal of Research and Practice, 26*(7–8), 629–644.

Baldwin, R. G., and Chronister, J. L. (2001). *Teaching without tenure: Policies and practices for a new era.* Baltimore: Johns Hopkins University Press.

Bartholomew, S. S., and Sandholtz, J. H. (2009). Competing views of teaching in a school-university partnership. *Teaching and Teacher Evaluation: An International Journal of Research and Studies, 25*(1), 155–165.

Baus, F., and Ramsbottom, C. A. (1999). Starting and sustaining a consortium. In L. G. Dotolo and J. T. Strandness (Eds.), *Best practices in higher education consortia: How institutions can work together.* New Directions for Higher Education, no. 106. San Francisco: Jossey-Bass.

Baxter, B. (2008). The power of partnership. *Community College Journal, 79*(2), 10–13.

Berger, P. L., and Luckmann, T. (1966). *The social construction of reality: A treatise in the sociology of knowledge.* New York: Doubleday.

Billett, S., Ovens, C., Clemans, A., and Seddon, T. (2007). Collaborative working and contested practices: Forming, developing and sustaining social partnerships in education. *Journal of Education Policy, 22*(6), 637–656.

Birnbaum, R. (2000). *Management fads in higher education.* San Francisco: Jossey-Bass.

Blumenstyk, G. (2009). In a time of crisis, colleges ought to be making history. *Chronicle of Higher Education, 55*(34), A1.

Boardman, C., and Bozeman, B. (2007). Role strain in university research centers. *Journal of Higher Education, 78*(4), 430–463.

Bolman, L. G., and Deal, T. E. (2008). *Reframing organizations: Artistry, choice, and leadership* (4th ed.). San Francisco: Jossey-Bass.

Bologna Declaration. (1999). *Bologna declaration.* Bologna, Italy: European Higher Education Area. Retrieved August 12, 2009, from http://www.ond.vlaanderen.be/hogeronder wijs/bologna/documents/MDC/BOLOGNA_DECLARATION1.pdf.

Boud, D., and Walker, D. (1993). Barriers to reflection on experience. In D. Boud, R. Cohen, and D. Walker (Eds.), *Reflection as a process of learning* (pp. 73–86). Bristol, PA: SRHE and Open University Press.

Bourdieu, P. (1983). Ökonomisches kapital, kulturelles kapital, soziales kapital. In R. Kreckel (Ed.), *Soziale Ungleichheiten (Soziale Welt, Sonderheft 2)* (pp. 183–198). Trans. R. Nice. Goettingen, Germany: Otto Schartz & Co. Retrieved December 10, 2009, from http://www9.georgetown.edu/faculty/irvinem/theory/Bourdieu-Forms_of_Capital.html.

Boyer, E. L. (1990). *Scholarship reconsidered: Priorities of the professoriate.* Lawrenceville, NJ: Princeton University Press.

Bracken, S. J. (2007). The importance of language, context, and communication as components of successful partnership. In M. J. Amey (Ed.), *Collaborations across educational sectors.* New Directions for Community Colleges, no. 139 (pp. 41–47). San Francisco: Jossey-Bass.

Bragg, D. D. (2000). Maximizing the benefits of tech-prep initiatives for high school students. In J. C. Palmer (Ed.), *How community colleges can create productive collaborations with local schools.* New Directions for Community Colleges, no. 111. San Francisco: Jossey-Bass.

Brewer, E. (2010). Leveraging partnerships to internationalize the liberal arts college: Campus internationalization and the faculty. In P. L. Eddy (Ed.), *International collaborations: Institutional frameworks and faculty roles.* New Directions for Higher Education, no. 150. San Francisco: Jossey-Bass.

Brewer, E., and Cunningham, K. (Eds.). (2010). *Integrating study abroad into the curriculum: Theory and practice across the disciplines.* Sterling, VA: Stylus.

Bridgwater, C. A., Bornstein, P. H., and Walkenbach, J. (1981). Ethical issues and the assignment of publication credit. *American Psychologist, 36,* 524–525.

Brookfield, S. D. (1995). *Becoming a critically reflective teacher.* San Francisco: Jossey-Bass.

Bryk, A. S., and Schneider, B. L. (2002). *Trust in schools: A core resource for improvement.* New York: Russell Sage Foundation.

Burns, J. M. (1978). *Leadership.* New York: Harper & Row.

Bushouse, B. K. (2005). Community nonprofit organizations and service-learning: Resource constraints to building partnerships with universities. *Michigan Journal of Community Service Learning, 12*(1), 32–40.

Cele, M. G. (2005). Meeting the knowledge needs of the academy and industry: A case study of a partnership between a university and a large energy company in South Africa. *Industry and Higher Education, 19*(2), 155–160.

Chamberlin, M., and Plucker, J. (2008). P–16 education: Where are we going? Where have we been? *Phi Delta Kappan, 89*(7), 472–479.

Chang, W., and Cha, M. (2008). Government driven partnership for lifelong learning in Korea: A case study of four cities. *International Journal of Lifelong Education, 27*(5), 579–597.

Childress, L. K. (2009). Internationalization plans for higher education institutions. *Journal of Studies in International Education, 13*(3), 289–309.

Chin, P., Bell, K. S., Munby, H., and Hutchinson, N. L. (2004). Epistemological appropriation in one high school student's learning in cooperative education. *American Educational Research Journal, 41*(2), 401–417.

Clark, B. R. (1972). The organizational saga in higher education. *Administrative Science Quarterly, 17*(2), 178–184.

Clifford, M., and Millar, S. B. (2008). *K–20 partnerships: Literature review and recommendations for research.* Madison: Wisconsin Center for Education Research, School of Education, University of Wisconsin–Madison.

Coburn, C. E., Bae, S., and Turner, E. O. (2008). Authority, status, and the dynamics of insider-outsider partnerships at the district level. *Peabody Journal of Education, 83*(3), 364–399.

Cohen, A. M., and Brawer, F. B. (2008). *The American community college* (5th ed.). San Francisco: Jossey-Bass.

Coleman, J. S. (1988). Social capital in the creation of human capital. *American Journal of Sociology, 94*, S95–S120.

College Board. (2009). *Trends in college pricing.* Princeton, NJ: College Board.

Connolly, M., Jones, C., and Jones, N. (2007). Managing collaboration across further and higher education: A case in practice. *Journal of Further and Higher Education, 31*(2), 159–169.

Cooper, J., and Mitsunaga, R. (2010). Faculty perspectives on international education: The nested realities of faculty collaborations. In P. L. Eddy (Ed.), *International collaborations: Institutional frameworks and faculty roles.* New Directions for Higher Education, no. 150. San Francisco: Jossey-Bass.

Creamer, E. G. (1999). Knowledge production, publication productivity, and the intimate academic partnerships. *Journal of Higher Education, 70*(3), 261–277.

Creamer, E. G. (2004). Assessing outcomes of long-term research collaboration. *Canadian Journal of Higher Education, 34*, 27–46.

Creamer, E. G. (2005). Promoting the effective evaluation of collaboratively produced scholarship: A call to action. In E. G. Creamer and L. R. Lattuca (Eds.), *Advancing faculty learning through interdisciplinary collaboration.* New Directions in Teaching and Learning, no. 102. San Francisco: Jossey-Bass.

Dallmer, D. (2004). Collaborative relationships in teacher education: A personal narrative of conflicting roles. *Curriculum Inquiry, 34*(1), 29–45.

Damrosch, D. (2000). *Meetings of the mind.* Princeton, NJ: Princeton University Press.

Daniel, D. E. (2002). Partnerships are essential to fundraising. *Community College Journal, 72*(4), 15.

Davies, G. K. (2006). *Setting a public agenda for higher education in the states.* Denver: Education Commission of the States.

de Wit, H. (2002). *Internationalization of higher education in the United States of America and Europe: A historical, comparative, and conceptual analysis.* Westport, CN.: Greenwood Press.

Diab, D. (2006). Strategic partnerships in fuel cell development. *Community College Journal of Research and Practice, 30*(2), 173–174.

Dickie, C., and Dickie, L. (2009). Alliance performance to integrate higher education: Smarter partners with shared values and capacity building. *US–China Education Review, 6*(7), 18–28.

Dominguez, R. (2006). Partnership, preparation, and progress in training community college administrative leaders. *Educational Considerations, 33*(2), 30–34.

Dorger, M. (1999). Cooperation for cost-effectiveness in purchasing. In L. G. Dotolo and J. T. Strandness (Eds.), *Best practices in higher education consortia: How institutions can work together.* New Directions for Higher Education, no. 106. San Francisco: Jossey-Bass.

Dovey, K. (2009). The role of trust in innovation. *Learning Organization, 16*(4), 311–325.

Dubetz, N., Lawrence, A., and Gningue, S. (2002). Formalizing a process for identifying urban PDS partnerships. *Issues in Teacher Education, 11*(2), 17–30.

Eddy, P. L. (2003). Sensemaking on campus: How community college presidents frame change. *Community College Journal of Research and Practice, 27*(6), 453–471.

Eddy, P. L. (2007). Alliances among community colleges: Odd bedfellows or lasting partners? In M. J. Amey (Ed.), *Collaborations across educational sectors.* New Directions for Community Colleges, no. 139. San Francisco: Jossey-Bass.

Eddy, P. L. (2010a). Institutional collaborations in Ireland: Leveraging an increased international presence. In P. L. Eddy (Ed.), *International collaborations: Institutional frameworks and faculty roles.* New Directions for Higher Education, no. 150. San Francisco: Jossey-Bass.

Eddy, P. L. (2010b). *Partnerships and Collaborations in Higher Education.* ASHE Higher Education Report, Vol. 36, No. 2. San Francisco: Jossey-Bass.

Eddy, P. L., and Gayle, J. G. (2008). New faculty on the block: Issues of stress and support. *Journal of Human Behavior in the Social Environment, 17*(1–2), 89–106.

Edens, R., and Gilsinan, J. F. (2005). Rethinking school partnerships. *Education and Urban Society, 37*(2), 123–138.

Eggins, H. (2003). Globalization and reform: Necessary conjunctions in higher education. In H. Eggins (Ed.), *Globalization and reform in higher education* (pp. 1–8). Berkshire, UK: Open University Press, 2003.

Etzioni, A. (1964). *Modern organizations.* New York: Prentice Hall.

Ewell, P. T. (2004). From the states. Tomorrow the world: Learning outcomes and the Bologna process. *Assessment Update, 16*(6), 11–13.

Fahey, C., Ihle, P., Macary, S., and O'Callahan, C. (2007). Opportunity knocks: A Connecticut school-community partnership closes the door on preschool expulsion. *Young Children, 62*(2), 21–24.

Fairhurst, G. T., and Sarr, R. A. (1996). *The art of framing: Managing the language of leadership.* San Francisco: Jossey-Bass.

Fairweather, J. S. (2005). Beyond the rhetoric: Trends in the relative value of teaching and research in faculty salaries. *Journal of Higher Education, 76*(4), 401–422.

Fang, S. C., and Hung, R.Y.Y. (2008). *Social capital, organizational learning capability, and technological knowledge transfer.* Paper presented at the Academy of Human Resource Development International Research Conference in the Americas, February, Panama City, FL.

Farrell, P. L., and Seifert, K. A. (2007). Lessons learned from a dual-enrollment partnership. In M. J. Amey (Ed.), *Collaborations across educational sectors.* New Directions for Community Colleges, no. 139. San Francisco: Jossey-Bass.

Fiedler, F. E. (1967). *A theory of leadership effectiveness.* New York: McGraw-Hill.

Finkelstein, M. J., Walker, E., and Chen, R. (2009). *The internationalization of the American faculty: Where are we? What drives or deters us?* Unpublished report. South Orange, NJ: Seton Hall University.

Fischer, K. (2009). U.S. colleges get serious with partners overseas. *Chronicle of Higher Education, 55*(25), A1.

Fluharty, C. W. (2007). *Written statement for the record before the United States House of Representatives, Committee on Agriculture, Subcommittee on Specialty Crops, Rural Development, and Foreign Agriculture.* Washington, DC. Retrieved April 15, 2008, from http://www.rupri.org/Forms/testimony032107.pdf.

Fowler, F. (2009). *Policy studies for educational leaders: An introduction* (3rd ed.). Boston: Allyn & Bacon.

Fraser, S. P. (2006). Shaping the university curriculum through partnerships and critical conversations. *International Journal for Academic Development, 11*(1), 5–11.

French, J.P.R., Jr., and Raven, B. (1960). The bases of social power. In D. Cartwright and A. Zander (Eds.), *Group dynamics* (pp. 607–623). New York: Harper & Row.

Frierson-Campbell, C. (2003). *Sound ways of learning: Anchoring music education to the PDS P–16 reform movement.* Paper presented at the Annual National Professional Development School Conference, March, Baltimore, MD.

Fullan, M. (2001). *Leading in a culture of change.* San Francisco: Jossey-Bass.

Fullan, M. (2002). The change leader. *Educational Leadership, 59*(8), 16–20.

Gappa, J. M., Austin, A. E., and Trice, A. G. (2007). *Rethinking faculty work: Higher education's strategic imperative.* San Francisco: Jossey-Bass.

Gillespie, R. (1993). *Manufacturing knowledge: A history of the Hawthorne studies.* Cambridge, UK: Press Syndicate of the University of Cambridge.

Gmelch, W. H., and Parkay, W. (1999). *Becoming a department chair: The transition from scholar to administrator.* Paper presented at the Annual Meeting of the American Educational Research Association, April, Montreal, QC.

Godbey, G. C., and Richter, G. J. (1999). Technology, consortia, and the relationship revolution in education. In L. G. Dotolo and J. T. Strandness (Eds.), *Best practices in higher education consortia: How institutions can work together.* New Directions for Higher Education, no. 106. San Francisco: Jossey-Bass.

Goduto, L. R., Doolittle, G., and Leake, D. (2008). Forming collaborative partnerships on a statewide level to develop quality school leaders. *Theory into Practice, 47*(4), 345–352.

Goleman, D. (2000). Leadership that gets results. *Harvard Business Review, 78*(2), 78–90.

Golfin, P. A. (1998). *Partnerships with community colleges: Vehicles to benefit Navy training and recruiting.* Alexandria, VA: CAN Corporation.

Granovetter, M. (1983). The strength of weak ties: A network theory revisited. *Sociology Theory, 1*, 201–233.

Gray, B. (1989). *Collaborating: Finding common ground for multiparty problems.* San Francisco: Jossey-Bass.

Grek, S., and Lawn, M. (2009). A short history of Europeanizing education: The new political work of calculating the future. *European Education, 41*(1), 32–54.

Griffin, T., and Curtin, P. (2007). *Regional partnerships at a glance. Revised.* Adelaide, Australia: National Centre for Vocational Education Research.

Hale, G. (2001). *Postsecondary options: Dual/concurrent enrollment.* Denver: Education Commission of the States.

Harmon, G., and Harmon, K. (2008). Strategic mergers of strong institutions to enhance competitive advantage. *Higher Education Policy, 21*(1), 99–121.

Harris, S. (2005). Professionals, partnerships and learning in changing times. *International Studies in Sociology of Education, 15*(1), 71–86.

Hatch, M. J., and Cunliffe, A. L. (2006). *Organization theory: Modern, symbolic, and postmodern perspectives.* New York: Oxford University Press.

Hay, S., and Kapitzke, C. (2009). Industry school partnerships: Reconstituting spaces of educational governance. *Globalisation, Societies and Education, 7*(2), 203–216.

Hazelkorn, E. (2009). The impact of global rankings on higher education research and the production of knowledge. *Reports 16.* Dublin, Ireland: Dublin Institute of Technology. Retrieved September 10, 2009, from http://arrow.dit.ie/cserrep/16.

Hebel, S. (2007). Partnership expands the college track. *Education Digest, 73*(2), 34–38.

Heffernan, T., and Poole, D. (2005). In search of 'the vibe': Creating effective international education partnerships. *Higher Education, 50*(2), 223–245.

Heifetz, R. (1994). *Leadership without easy answers.* Cambridge, MA: Harvard University Press.

Herzberg, F. (1959). *The motivation to work.* New York: Wiley.

Higher Education Authority. (2008). *Transformations: How research is changing Ireland.* Dublin, Ireland: Higher Education Authority.

Hinck, S. S., and others. (2009). Reflection and research: Forming the perfect FIT. *Teaching and Learning: The Journal of Natural Inquiry and Reflective Practice, 23*(3), 120–133.

Hirota, J. M. (2005). *Reframing education: The partnership strategy and public schools.* Chicago: Chapin Hall Center for Children.

Hodson, P. J., and Thomas, H. G. (2001). Higher education as an international commodity: Ensuring quality in partnerships. *Assessment & Evaluation in Higher Education, 26*(2), 101–112.

Hoff, D. L. (2002). School-business partnerships: It's the schools' turn to raise the grade! *School Community Journal, 12*(2), 63–78.

Holland, D. (2010). Notes from the field: Lessons learned in building a framework for an international collaboration. In P. L. Eddy (Ed.), *International collaborations: Institutional frameworks and faculty roles.* New Directions for Higher Education, no. 150. San Francisco: Jossey-Bass.

Holley, K. A. (2009). *Understanding interdisciplinary challenges and opportunities in higher education.* ASHE Higher Education Report, vol. 35, no. 2. San Francisco: Jossey-Bass.

Huckabee, C. (2008, October 8). American institutions top British list of world's best international universities. *Chronicle of Higher Education*. Retrieved December 18, 2009, from http://chronicle.com/article/American-Institutions-Top-B/41771/.

Hvistendahl, M. (2009). Renewed attention to social sciences in China leads to new partnerships with American universities. *Chronicle of Higher Education, 55*(23), A35.

Illinois State Department of Human Resources. (2001). *Guidebook to developing a collaborative partnership written agreement*. East St. Louis, IL: Illinois Head Start State Collaboration Office.

Jie, Y. (2010). International partnerships: A game theory perspective. In P. L. Eddy (Ed.), *International collaborations: Institutional frameworks and faculty roles*. New Directions for Higher Education no. 150. San Francisco: Jossey-Bass.

Johnson, C. (2007). *The role of social capital in creating sustainable partnerships*. Unpublished dissertation. Mt. Pleasant: Central Michigan University.

John-Steiner, V. (2000). *Creative collaboration*. Oxford and New York: Oxford University Press.

Johnston, H. (2009). Dancing partners: Schools and Businesses. *School Administrator, 9*(66), 24–28.

Johnston, S. W., and Noftsinger, J. B., Jr. (2004). *Getting a grip on strategic alliances*. Washington, DC: Association of Governing Boards of Universities and Colleges.

Kearney, K. S., and others. (2007). Building an academe and government partnership in workforce education: Challenges and possibilities. *Journal of Industrial Teacher Education, 44*(3), 71–91.

Kelman, H. (1961). Process of opinion change. *Public Opinion Quarterly, 25*(1), 57–78.

Kisker, C. B. (2005). Creating and sustaining community college–university transfer partnerships: A qualitative case study. Paper presented at the annual meeting of the Association for the Study of Higher Education, November, Philadelphia, PA.

Kisker, C. B., and Carducci, R. (2003). UCLA community college partnerships with the private sector: Organizational contexts and models for successful collaboration. *Community College Review, 31*(3), 55–74.

Kisker, C. B., and Hauser, P. (2007). Partnering to move students into college and community-oriented careers: The administration of justice department at East Los Angeles College. In M. J. Amey (Ed.), *Collaborations across educational sectors*. New Directions for Community Colleges, no. 139. San Francisco: Jossey-Bass.

Kolowich, S. (2009, December). Another one bites the dust. *Inside Higher Education,* 1–2. Retrieved December 10, 2009, from http://www.insidehighered.com/layout/set/print/news/2009/12/09/u21.

Kotter, J. P. (2008). *A sense of urgency*. Boston: Harvard Business Press.

Kotter, J. P., and Cohen, D. S. (2002). *The heart of change: Real-life stories of how people change their organizations*. Cambridge, MA: Harvard Business School Press.

Krasnow, M. H. (1997). *Learning to listen, talk and trust: Constructing collaborations*. Paper presented at an annual meeting of the American Educational Research Association, March, Chicago, IL.

Kreuger, C. (2006). *Dual enrollment: Policy issues confronting state policymakers.* Denver: Education Commission of the States.

Kruss, G. (2006). Working partnerships: The challenge of creating mutual benefit for academics and industry. *Perspectives in Education, 24*(3), 1–13.

Labi, A. (January, 2009a). European institutions lead in international dual-degree partnerships, study finds. *Chronicle of Higher Education, 55*(22), A26.

Labi, A. (September, 2009b). American graduate programs with overseas partners are on the rise. *Chronicle of Higher Education.* Retrieved September 21, 2009, from http://chronicle.com/article/American-Graduate-Programs-/48529/.

Lacey, R. A., and Kingsley, C. (1988). *A guide to working partnerships.* Waltham, MA: Center for Human Resources, Brandeis University.

Lang, D. W. (2003). The future of merger: What do we want mergers to do—efficiency or diversity? *Canadian Journal of Higher Education, 33*(3), 19–46.

Lattuca, L. (2001). *Creating interdisciplinarity: Interdisciplinary research and teaching among college and university faculty.* Nashville, TN: Vanderbilt University Press.

Lattuca, L. R., and Creamer, E. G. (2005). Learning as professional practice. In E. G. Creamer and L. R. Lattuca (Eds.), *Advancing faculty learning through interdisciplinary collaboration.* New Directions in Teaching and Learning, no. 102. San Francisco: Jossey-Bass.

Lefever-Davis, S., Johnson, C., and Pearman, C. (2007). Two sides of a partnership: Egalitarianism and empowerment in school-university partnerships. *Journal of Educational Research, 100*(4), 204–210.

Lemaire, I., Knapp, J. A., and Lowe, S. (2008). Collaborating on state-level institutional research in New Hampshire. In R. K. Toutkoushian and T. R. Massa (Eds.), *Conducting institutional research in non-campus-based settings.* New Directions for Institutional Research, no. 139. San Francisco: Jossey-Bass.

Leskes, A. (2006). Leading through the perfect storm. *Liberal Education, 92*(1), 28–33.

Leslie, D. W., and Fretwell, E. K., Jr. (1996). *Wise moves in hard times: Creating and managing resilient colleges and universities.* San Francisco: Jossey-Bass.

Lewin K. (1943/1997). Defining the "field at a given time." *Psychological Review,* 50, 292–310. Republished in *Resolving Social Conflicts and Field Theory in Social Science.* Washington, DC: American Psychological Association.

Lindstrom, L. E., and others. (2009). Building employment training partnerships between vocational rehabilitation and community colleges. *Rehabilitation Counseling Bulletin, 52*(3), 189–201.

Livingston, J. A. (1997). *Metacognition: An overview.* Unpublished manuscript. Buffalo, State University of New York at Buffalo. Retrieved December 28, 2009, from http://www.gse.buffalo.edu/fas/shuell/cep564/Metacog.htm.

Maeroff, G. I., Callan, P. M., and Usdan, M. D. (Eds.). (2001). *The learning connection: New partnerships between schools and colleges.* New York: Teachers College Press.

Maimon, E. P. (2006). The university as public square. *Presidency, 9*(3), 26–31.

Maldonado-Maldonada, A., and Cantwell, B. (2008). Caught on the Mexican-U.S. border: The insecurity and desire of collaboration between two universities. *Comparative Education, 44*(3), 317–331.

McCord, R. S. (2002). Breaking the school district boundaries: Collaboration and cooperation for success. *Education, 123,* 386–389.

McGinn, M. K., and others. (2005). Living ethics: A narrative of collaboration and belonging in a research team. *Reflective Practice, 6,* 551–567.

McMurtrie, B., and Wheeler, D. (2008). Leaders urge colleges to think globally despite economic crisis. *Chronicle of Higher Education, 55*(13), A25.

Mendoza, P., and Berger, J. B. (2008). Academic capitalism and academic culture: A case study. *Educational Policy Analysis, 16*(23), 1–27.

Miller, P. (2005). Dialogue facilitating collaboration: A critical perspective. *Journal of School Public Relations, 26*(1), 21–34.

Mooney, P. (2008). An American college in China struggles to deliver. *Chronicle of Higher Education, 54*(34), A1.

Morgan, G. (2006). *Images of organization.* Thousand Oaks, CA: Sage.

Morrison, M. C. (2008). The strategic value of dual enrollment programs. *Techniques: Connecting Education and Careers, 83*(7), 26–27.

National Commission on Excellence in Education. (1983). *A nation at risk.* Washington, DC: Government Printing Office.

Neumann, A. (1995). On the making of hard times and good times. *Journal of Higher Education, 66*(1), 3–31.

Neumann, A. (2009). Protecting the passion of scholars in times of change. *Change: The Magazine of Higher Learning, 41*(2), 10–15.

Oh, J. E. (2008). Equity of the Bologna system. *European Education, 40*(1), 35–50.

O'Hara, S. (2009). Internationalizing the academy: The impact of scholar mobility. In R. Bhandari and S. Laughlin (Eds.), *Higher education on the move: New developments in global mobility* (pp. 29–48). New York: Institute of International Education.

Olson, L. (2006). States striving to build data systems across education levels. *Education Week, 25*(41), 17.

O'Meara, K. A., Terosky, A. L., and Neumann, A. (2009). *Faculty careers and work lives: A professional growth perspective.* ASHE Higher Education Report, vol. 34, no. 3. San Francisco: Jossey-Bass.

Patterson, G. (2005). Collaboration/competition crossroads: National/supranational tertiary education policies on a collision course. *Tertiary Education and Management, 11*(4), 355–368.

Patterson, L. D. (1970). *Consortia in American higher education.* Washington, DC: ERIC Clearinghouse on Higher Education.

Peterson, M. W. (1998). *Improvement to emergence: An organization-environment research agenda for a postsecondary knowledge industry.* Stanford, CA: National Center for Postsecondary Improvement.

Pick, D. (2003). Framing and frame shifting in a higher education merger. *Tertiary Education and Management, 9*(4), 299–316.

Poole, M. S., and Van de Ven, A. H. (2004). *Handbook of organizational change and innovation*. Oxford, UK: Oxford University Press.

Prigge, G. W. (2005). University-industry partnerships: What do they mean to universities? A review of the literature. *Industry and Higher Education, 19*(3), 221–229.

Putnam, R. D. (2000). *Bowling alone: The collapse and revival of American community*. New York: Simon & Schuster.

Reed, G. G., Cooper, J. E., and Young, L. (2007). A partnership in flux: The demise of a program. In M. J. Amey (Ed.), *Collaborations across educational sectors*. New Directions for Community Colleges, no. 139. San Francisco: Jossey-Bass.

Reyes, P., Alexander, C., and Diem, S. (2008). Trust and school reform implementation. *Journal of School Public Relations, 29*(2), 237–275.

Rochford, K. A., O'Neill, A., Gelb, A., and Ross, K. J. (2005). *P–16: The last education reform. Book one: Reflections on school restructuring and the establishment of local preschool through college compacts*. Canton, OH: Stark Education Partnership.

Rochford, K. A., O'Neill, A., Gelb, A., and Ross, K. J. (2007). *P–16: The last education reform. Book two: Emerging local, regional, and state efforts*. Canton, OH: Stark Education Partnership.

Rost, J. C. (1991). *Leadership for the twenty-first century*. New York: Praeger.

Russell, J. F., and Flynn, R. B. (2000). Commonalities across effective collaboratives. *Peabody Journal of Education, 75*(3), 196–204.

Saito, E., Imansyah, H., Kubok, I., and Hendayana, S. (2007). A study of the partnership between schools and universities to improve science and mathematics education in Indonesia. *International Journal of Educational Development, 27*(2), 194–204.

Saltmarsh, J., Giles, D. E., Jr., Ward, E., and Buglione, S. M. (2009). Rewarding community-engaged scholarship. *Rewarding community-engaged scholarship*. New Directions for Higher Education, no. 147. San Francisco: Jossey-Bass.

Sandy, M., and Holland, B. A. (2006). Different worlds and common ground: Community partner perspectives on campus-community partnerships. *Michigan Journal of Community Service Learning, 13*(1), 30–43.

Scarino, A., Crichton, J., and Woods, M. (2007). The role of language and culture in open learning in international collaborative programmes. *Open Learning, 22*(3), 219–233.

Schön, D. A., and Rein, M. (1994). *Frame reflection: Toward the resolution of intractable policy controversies*. New York: Basic Books.

Scott, J. (1988). Social network analysis. *Sociology, 22*(1), 109–127.

Sebalj, D., Hudson, S., Ryan, J., and Wight-Boycott, J. (2007). Alliance through change. *Journal of Higher Education Policy and Management, 29*(3), 275–287.

Shanghai Jiao Tong University. (2009). *Academic ranking of world universities*. Shanghai, China: Shanghai Jiao Tong University. Retrieved December 28, 2009, from http://www.arwu.org/.

Shapiro, B. (2002). Higher education in the new century: Some history, some challenges. *Education Canada, 42*(1), 12–15.

Shinners, K. D. (2006). Follow the leader: Project structure and leadership roles in a grant-supported collaboration. *International Journal of Educational Management, 29*(3), 206–214.

Silka, L. (2008). Down under, higher education drives economic development. *New England Journal of Higher Education, 23*(2), 21–22.

Sink, D. W., Jackson, K. L., Boham, K. A., and Shockley, D. (2004). The Western North Carolina Technology Consortium: A collaborative approach to bridging the digital divide. *Community College Journal of Research and Practice, 28*(4), 321–329.

Slaughter, S., and Rhoades, G. (2004). *Academic capitalism and the new economy: Markets, state, and higher education.* Baltimore: Johns Hopkins University Press.

Sorcinelli, M. D. (2000). *Principles of good practice. Supporting early-career faculty: Guidance for deans, department chairs, and other academic leaders.* Washington, DC: American Association for Higher Education.

Spiegel, D., and Keith-Spiegel, P. (1970). Assignment of publication credits: Ethics and practices of psychologists. *American Psychologist, 25,* 738–747.

Stensakera, B., and Harvey, L. (2006). Old wine in new bottles? A comparison of public and private accreditation schemes in higher education. *Higher Education Policy, 19*(1), 65–85.

Stephens, D., and Boldt, G. (2004). School/university partnerships: Rhetoric, reality, and intimacy. *Phi Delta Kappan, 85*(9), 703.

Tafel, J., and Eberhart, N. (1999). *Statewide school-college (K–16) partnerships to improve student performance. State strategies that support successful student transitions from secondary to postsecondary education.* Denver: State Higher Education Executive Officers.

Tedrow, B., and Mabokela, R. (2007). An analysis of international partnership programs: The case of an historically disadvantaged institution in South Africa. *Higher Education, 54,* 159–179.

Temple, P. (2006). Creating social capital: The impact of international programmes on Polish and Romanian higher education. *Tertiary Education and Management, 12*(1), 1–20.

Tennant, M., and Pogson, P. (1995). *Learning and change in the adult years: A developmental perspective.* San Francisco: Jossey-Bass.

Thornton, R. H., and Shattuck, J. M. (2006). Workforce development alliances. *Community College Journal of Research and Practice, 30*(2), 165–167.

Tierney, W. (1991). *Culture and ideology in higher education.* New York: Praeger.

Tirronen, J., and Nokkala, T. (2009). Structural development of Finnish universities: Achieving competitiveness and academic excellence. *Higher Education Quarterly, 63*(3), 219–236.

Townsend, B. K., and Twombly, S. B. (2007). *Community college faculty: Overlooked and undervalued.* ASHE-ERIC Higher Education Report, vol. 32, no. 6. San Francisco: Jossey-Bass.

Tuckman, B. W. (1965). Developmental sequence in small groups. *Psychological Bulletin, 63,* 384–399.

Turner, Y., and Robson, S. (2008). *Internationalizing the university.* London: Continuum International Publishing Group.

U.S. Department of Education. (2006). *A test of leadership: Charting the future of U.S. higher education. A report of the commission appointed by Secretary of Education Margaret Spellings.* Washington, DC: U.S. Department of Education.

Useem, M. (2003). *Leading up: How to lead your boss so you both win*. New York: Three Rivers Press.

Van de Ven, A. H., and Poole, M. S. (1995). Explaining development and change in organizations. *Academy of Management Review, 20*, 510–540.

Van de Water, G., and Rainwater, T. (2001). *What is P–16 education? A primer for legislators*. Denver: Education Commission of the States.

Vaughn, J. C. (2009). AAU and ARL: The role of partnerships and collective advocacy in policy development. *Libraries and the Academy, 9*(3), 397–404.

Walton, J. S., and Guarisco, G. (2007). Structural issues and knowledge management in transnational education partnerships. *Journal of European Industrial Training, 31*(5), 358–376.

Warren, L. L., and Peel, H. A. (2005). Collaborative model for school reform through a rural school/university partnership. *Education, 126*(2), 346–352.

Watson, A., and Jordan, L. (1999). Economic development and consortia. In L. G. Dotolo and J. T. Strandness (Eds.), *Best practices in higher education consortia: How institutions can work together*. New Directions for Higher Education, no. 106. San Francisco: Jossey-Bass.

Watson, J. S. (2007). Stepping outside the big box high school: A partnership influenced by goals, capital, and decision-making. In M. J. Amey (Ed.), *Collaborations across educational sectors*. New Directions for Community Colleges, no. 139. San Francisco: Jossey-Bass.

Weber, M. (2009). *From Max Weber: Essays in sociology*. New York: Routledge.

Weick, K. E. (1976). Educational organizations as loosely coupled systems. *Administrative Science Quarterly, 21*(1), 1–19.

Weick, K. E. (1995). *Sensemaking in organizations*. Thousand Oaks, CA: Sage.

Welty, J. D., and Lukens, M. (2009). Partnering with state government to transform a region. *Metropolitan Universities, 20*(1), 59–74.

Widmayer, P. (1999). Statewide consortia for the use of technology. In L. G. Dotolo and J. T. Strandness (Eds.), *Best practices in higher education consortia: How institutions can work together*. New Directions for Higher Education, no. 106. San Francisco: Jossey-Bass.

Willis, M. (2006). Why do Chinese universities seek foreign university partners? An investigation of the motivating factors behind a significant area of alliance activity. *Journal of Marketing for Higher Education, 16*(1), 115–141.

Willis, M. (2008). An identification and evaluation of the various types and forms of personal relationships with a Sino foreign university strategic alliance context. *Journal of Teaching in International Business, 19*(3), 222–245.

Wood, J. T. (1996). Communication and relational culture. In K. M. Galvin and P. Cooper (Eds.), *Making connections: Readings in relational communication* (pp. 11–15). Los Angeles: Roxbury Publishing.

Worrall, L. (2007). Asking the community: A case study of community partner perspectives. *Michigan Journal of Community Service Learning, 14*(1), 5–17.

Yff, J. (1996). *State policies to promote P–16 collaboration: A survey of professional development and P–12 content standards*. Washington, DC: American Association of Colleges for Teacher Education.

Zahn, G., Sandell, E., and Lindsay, C. (2007). Fostering global-mindedness in teacher preparation. *International Journal of Teaching and Learning in Higher Education, 19*(3), 331–335.

Zakocs, R. C., Tiwari, R., Vehige, T., and DeJong, W. (2008). Roles of organizers and champions in building campus-community prevention partnerships. *Journal of American College Health, 57*(2), 233–241.

Zeelen, J., and van der Linden, J. (2009). Capacity building in Southern Africa. Experiences and reflections—Towards joint knowledge production and social change in international development cooperation. *Compare: A Journal of Comparative and International Education, 39*(5), 615–628.

Zimpher, N. L. (2002). Partnering for systemic change. *Metropolitan Universities: An International Forum, 13*(4), 137–157.

Name Index

A

Acker, J., 45
Adler, P. S., 59
Alexander, C., 18
Allen-Gil, S., 68
Altbach, P. G., 10, 76
Amey, M. J., 1, 11, 14, 38–39, 62, 63, 65, 74, 78, 80
Anderson, R. D., 6
Astin, A., 24
Astin, H., 24
Austin, A. E., 2, 11, 56, 57, 59, 62, 86

B

Bae, S., 34
Baker, G. A. III, 8
Baldwin, R. G., 11, 56, 57, 59, 62, 86
Bartholomew, S. S., 7
Baus, F., 20, 50, 51, 69, 80, 81
Baxter, B., 4
Bell, K. S., 7
Berger, J. B., 8, 60
Berger, P. L., 45
Billett, S., 72
Birnbaum, R., 79
Blumenstyk, G., 14
Boardman, C., 62
Boham, K. A., 22
Boldt, G., 59
Bolman, L. G., 35, 36, 39
Bornstein, P. H., 59
Boud, D., 58

Bourdieu, P., 29
Boyer, E. L., 56, 87
Bozeman, B., 62
Bracken, S. J., 18
Bragg, D. D., 7
Brawer, F. B., 7, 58
Brewer, E., 76, 78
Bridgwater, C. A., 59
Brookfield, S. D., 58
Brown, D. F., 38–39, 62, 80
Bryk, A. S., 59
Buglione, S. M., 80
Burns, J. M., 80
Bushouse, B. K., 48

C

Callan, P. M., 4
Campbell, T., 11
Cantwell, B., 76
Carducci, R., 8
Cele, M. G., 28
Cha, M., 72
Chamberlin, M., 13
Chang, W., 72
Chen, R., 9, 73
Childress, L. K., 77
Chin, P., 7
Chronister, J. L., 56
Clark, B. R., 38, 82
Clemans, A., 72
Clifford, M., 4, 8
Coburn, C. E., 34

Heifetz, R., 37, 51
Hendayana, S., 75
Herzberg, F., 22
Hinck, S. S., 59, 86
Hirota, J. M., 4
Hodson, P. J., 73
Hoff, D. L., 23
Holland, B. A., 7
Holland, D., 14, 74
Holley, K. A., 2, 11, 12, 59, 62
Huckabee, C., 12
Hudson, S., 69, 81
Hung, R.Y.Y., 33
Hutchinson, N. L., 7
Hvistendahl, M., 77

I

Ihle, P., 23
Imansyah, H., 75

J

Jackson, K. L., 22
Jie, Y., 85
Johnson, C., 2, 19
John-Steiner, V., 58, 59
Johnston, H., 18, 69
Johnston, S. W., 23, 69, 72
Jones, C., 5
Jones, N., 5
Jordan, L., 22

K

Kapitzke, C., 74
Kearney, K. S., 5
Keith-Spiegel, P., 59
Kelman, H., 28, 32, 36, 37, 38, 40, 68, 80
Kingsley, C., 24, 25
Kisker, C. B., 7, 8
Knapp, J. A., 9
Kolowich, S., 78
Kotter, J. P., 24, 25, 26, 38, 78, 79, 80, 87
Krasnow, M. H., 20
Kreuger, C., 6, 7
Kruss, G., 5, 9
Kubok, I., 75
Kwon, S., 59

L

Labi, A., 12, 73, 76, 77
Lacey, R. A., 24, 25
Lang, D. W., 69
Lattuca, L. R., 11, 19, 57, 63, 86
Lawn, M., 70
Lawrence, A., 60
Leake, D., 58
Lefever-Davis, S., 2
Lemaire, I., 9
Leskes, A., 1, 14
Leslie, D. W., 24
Lewin, K., 26, 52
Lindsay, C., 73
Lindstrom, L. E., 7
Livingston, J. A., 58
Lowe, S., 9
Luckmann, T., 45
Lukens, M., 72

M

Mabokela, R., 74, 75
Macary, S., 23
Maeroff, G. I., 4
Maimon, E. P., 1
Maldonado-Maldonada, A., 76
McCord, R. S., 8
McGinn, M. K., 59
McMurtrie, B., 9
Mendoza, P., 8, 60
Millar, S. B., 4, 8
Miller, P., 49
Mitsunaga, R., 11, 19, 28, 40, 62, 74
Mooney, P., 12
Morgan, G., 30, 37, 41, 45, 46, 47, 59, 63, 80
Morrison, M. C., 6
Munby, H., 7

N

Neumann, A., 35, 38, 44, 62, 64, 82, 87
Noftsinger, J. B. Jr., 23, 69, 72
Nokkala, T., 69

Subject Index

41–42; social capital of the champion, 27–49; structural factors defining the stage of action, 45–46; success factors, 5; symbolism, 45; technology, control of, 44; uncertainty, ability to cope with, 43–44

Policy agenda, setting for educational partnerships, 72–73

Policymakers: and educational partnerships, 88; and mandates for collaboration, 14

Pooling resources, 21; creation of consortia for, 69

Power, 40–41; sources of (Morgan), 46–47

Power sources, 46–47

Professional development schools, 59–60

Program collaboration, 62

Q

Queensland University of Technology, and economic development, 6

R

Reform, educational, 4–5

Relationship building: educational partnerships, 80–81; international educational partnerships, 75

Relationships, and social capital, 30–32

Resource savings, and educational partnerships, 7–8

Resources, 46–48; pooling, 21, 69, scarce, 41–42

S

S-W-O-T analysis, 79

Sabbatical leaves, and educational partnerships, 73

Scarce resources, control of, 41–42

Seamless educational systems: and reform effort, 5; work on, 14

Second-order change, 26

Shanghai Jiao Tong University, 76

Sharing expenses for technology, 22

Social capital, 10–11; of the champion, 27–47; and information channels, 30; levels of, held by each partner, 29; relationships inherent in, 30–32; and trust, 29–30, 34; visualizing, 32

Social network analysis, 32–34; example of, 33

Space: adaptive, 51; group, 59

Spellings Report, 4, 70

Student learning, and educational partnerships, 7

Symbolism, partnerships, 45

T

Tangible resources, 46–47

Tech Prep, 23

Technology, control of, 44

Technology preparation programs, 7

TRIO, 7

Trust: partnerships built on, 5, and social capital, 29–30, 34

U

Uncertainty, 43–44

Uncertainty, ability to cope with, 43–44

Upward Bound, 7

U.S. Department of Education, 4, 70

V

Ventures, joint, *See* Joint ventures

Visualizing social capital, 32

Vocational training programs, in community colleges, 7

W

Webster, Duane, 9

Workforce training programs, 23

About the Author

Pamela L. Eddy is associate professor of higher education in educational policy, planning, and leadership at the College of William and Mary. She received her M.S. in resource economics from Cornell University and her Ph.D. from the Higher, Adult, and Lifelong Education Department at Michigan State University. Her research interests include academic culture and organization in higher education, gender issues, and community college leadership. Eddy has worked in continuing education in both two- and four-year institutions.

About the ASHE Higher Education Report Series

Since 1983, the ASHE (formerly ASHE-ERIC) Higher Education Report Series has been providing researchers, scholars, and practitioners with timely and substantive information on the critical issues facing higher education. Each monograph presents a definitive analysis of a higher education problem or issue, based on a thorough synthesis of significant literature and institutional experiences. Topics range from planning to diversity and multiculturalism, to performance indicators, to curricular innovations. The mission of the Series is to link the best of higher education research and practice to inform decision making and policy. The reports connect conventional wisdom with research and are designed to help busy individuals keep up with the higher education literature. Authors are scholars and practitioners in the academic community. Each report includes an executive summary, review of the pertinent literature, descriptions of effective educational practices, and a summary of key issues to keep in mind to improve educational policies and practice.

The Series is one of the most peer reviewed in higher education. A National Advisory Board made up of ASHE members reviews proposals. A National Review Board of ASHE scholars and practitioners reviews completed manuscripts. Six monographs are published each year and they are approximately 120 pages in length. The reports are widely disseminated through Jossey-Bass and John Wiley & Sons, and they are available online to subscribing institutions through Wiley InterScience (http://www.interscience.wiley.com).

Call for Proposals

The ASHE Higher Education Report Series is actively looking for proposals. We encourage you to contact one of the editors, Dr. Kelly Ward (kaward@wsu.edu) or Dr. Lisa Wolf-Wendel (lwolf@ku.edu), with your ideas.

Recent Titles

ORDER FORM SUBSCRIPTION AND SINGLE ISSUES

DISCOUNTED BACK ISSUES:

Use this form to receive 20% off all back issues of *ASHE Higher Education Report.*
All single issues priced at **$23.20** (normally $29.00)

TITLE	ISSUE NO.	ISBN
_____	_____	_____
_____	_____	_____
_____	_____	_____

Call 888-378-2537 or see mailing instructions below. When calling, mention the promotional code JBXND to receive your discount. For a complete list of issues, please visit www.josseybass.com/go/aehe

SUBSCRIPTIONS: (1 YEAR, 6 ISSUES)

☐ New Order   ☐ Renewal

U.S.	☐ Individual: $174	☐ Institutional: $244
CANADA/MEXICO	☐ Individual: $174	☐ Institutional: $304
ALL OTHERS	☐ Individual: $210	☐ Institutional: $355

Call 888-378-2537 or see mailing and pricing instructions below.
Online subscriptions are available at www.interscience.wiley.com

ORDER TOTALS:

Issue / Subscription Amount: $ _____

Shipping Amount: $ _____
(for single issues only – subscription prices include shipping)

Total Amount: $ _____

SHIPPING CHARGES:

	SURFACE	DOMESTIC	CANADIAN
First Item	$5.00		$6.00
Each Add'l Item	$3.00		$1.50

(No sales tax for U.S. subscriptions. Canadian residents, add GST for subscription orders. Individual rate subscriptions must be paid by personal check or credit card. Individual rate subscriptions may not be resold as library copies.)

BILLING & SHIPPING INFORMATION:

☐ **PAYMENT ENCLOSED:** *(U.S. check or money order only. All payments must be in U.S. dollars.)*

☐ **CREDIT CARD:** ☐ VISA ☐ MC ☐ AMEX

Card number _____ Exp. Date _____

Card Holder Name _____ Card Issue # *(required)* _____

Signature _____ Day Phone _____

☐ **BILL ME:** *(U.S. institutional orders only. Purchase order required.)*

Purchase order # _____
                  Federal Tax ID 13559302 • GST 89102-8052

Name _____

Address _____

Phone _____ E-mail _____

Copy or detach page and send to: **John Wiley & Sons, PTSC, 5th Floor**
989 Market Street, San Francisco, CA 94103-1741

Order Form can also be faxed to: **888-481-2665**

PROMO JBXND

CPSIA information can be obtained at www.ICGtesting.com
Printed in the USA
LVOW05s0020260914

405919LV00009B/229/P